PLAY THE GAME

Bowls

Bowls

JAMES MEDLYCOTT

Hamlyn

London·New York·Sydney·Toronto

Contents

Acknowledgements

The photographs in this book are from the Hamlyn Picture Library with the exception of the following: All Sport (Steve Powell), cover; Central Press Photos Ltd, page 57; Hepworths Tailoring, page 61; Keystone Press Agency Ltd, page 16 (left); Sporting Pictures (UK) Ltd, end-papers, title page, page 52-3; Western Times Co Ltd, page 16 (right); the author, pages 10 (all three), 12 (top left and centre, lower left and centre), 13 (both), 25 (both), 30, 51 (both), 54-5

The diagrams were drawn by Lim Mei-Lan

Published by
The Hamlyn Publishing Group Limited
London · New York · Sydney · Toronto
Astronaut House, Feltham, Middlesex, England

ISBN 0 600 50016 0

Printed in Italy

Chapter One
Preparing to Play

Who can doubt that in pre-historic times man and his sons when out on walks picked up large stones and threw them at targets. Certainly there is ample evidence of ball and target games being played some 4,000 years BC.

Invention of the ball has been attributed to the Lydians and Homer wrote of Anagalla introducing Princess Nausica, daughter of the King Alcinous of Phoeacia, to the joys of playing with a ball.

Evolution is a slow process so not until the thirteenth century is there any sure record of people trundling large bowls at targets placed at the far end of a flat area of grass; playing bowls as we know it to-day.

The object was to deliver one's bowls nearer to the target than the opponents. The oldest existing green is at Southampton and it dates back to 1299.

This was a somewhat subtler game than the parallel and popular pastime, skittles. This still exists, either in its original name or as 'ten pin bowling', the object of both being to knock down the skittles at the far end of an alley.

Legend has it that the highly refined and constantly growing international game Lawn Bowls – the word 'Lawn' is not used in the British Isles – came into being through chance during the sixteenth century. Charles Brandon, the Duke of Suffolk, is reputed to have been contesting an exciting game when he delivered a bowl with such force that it shattered into several pieces.

Always a man or resource, he rushed indoors in search of a substitute. His quickly scanning eyes took in the decorative stairway and the banisters which ended in a large, ornamental ball. Calling for a handsaw, he soon separated it from its fixing and took it outside to resume play. However, in cutting it free the saw had flattened one side of the sphere, so setting up an imbalance that resulted in it travelling in a curve instead of the customary straight line of a perfect sphere.

Alert of mind and skilled in performance, he exploited this imbalance – in Lawn Bowls it is called 'bias' – of the substitute bowl by curling it round bowls in front of the target, so winning easily.

It is a romantic idea and, certainly, the inception of biassed bowls is fixed in the sixteenth century. Yet few historians would insist that 'that was the birth of Lawn Bowls.'

Despite the terrible things one reads in papers or hears on television and radio each day, British people generally are among the world leaders in sophistication. Consequently, they tend to prefer games which combine shrewd finesse with occasional force to those limited to 'brute force and blankety ignorance'. Bowls – to drop the 'Lawn' from now on – is high on any list of games that meet that specification. It is, additionally, one of the tiny minority of games in which age only becomes a handicap if it is accompanied by physical or mental disability. So there is nothing uncommon in three generations of one family competing together in one of the national, county or other competitions which abound in all bowls-playing countries.

This is one of the several reasons why Bowls is among the most widely played ball games in the British Isles and is certainly the most popular game in Australia and South Africa. It is growing rapidly in the USA especially among middle-aged and elderly people. Thanks in part to an alert English export group, BDNW, the game has spread to European countries and there are greens in such unlikely places as the roof of a skyscraper in Tokyo and another at a hotel in Fuengirola. If there ever should be a world 'Miss Bowls Contest' I fancy the Japanese would win it.

In Britain there are three codes of Bowls, Crown Green, Federation and Association. Of these the Association code is the one that conforms with the rules and conditions laid down by the International Bowling Board, the game's world governing organisation. Under their authorisation there have now been four World Championship series and more are scheduled to follow at four yearly intervals. The parallel body of the women's game, the Women's International Bowling Board, have also staged World Championships. Except in the USA, there is a tendency for sex 'apartheid' in bowls but the changing times are slowly helping to bring men and women together on the greens.

There is little difference between the Federation and Association code of bowls. Played mostly in East Anglia and the midlands, the Federation game allows smaller greens and it has no need of a ditch separating the green from the banks surrounding it.

Differences in rules relate primarily to details quickly learned when switching from the IBB game.

Crown green bowls differs considerably and there is a special section on the game later in this book.

The object of the game, be it staged as one against one (singles), two against two (pairs), three against three (triples), or four against four (fours), remains the same. Each player or side strives to deliver bowls so that they finish nearer to a small white ball, the jack, than those of the opposition. Each bowl that finishes nearer than the opposition's best bowl scores a point. The jack is delivered first towards the far end of a strip of the green. These strips are named 'rinks' and are approximately 18 feet wide.

The score is recorded after each player or group of players has delivered all his/their bowls from one end of the bowling green towards the jack at the other end of the green. After the score has been recorded the players deliver all their bowls back down the

Right: Bowl when viewed from behind.

Diagram 1: A bowl is biassed because one side is slightly flattened, so leaving the other side slightly heavier in weight. So as it rolls towards the ditch it will have two forces: forward (F) because of propulsion, sideways (S) because of bias (extra weight). If F remained constant, its resultant direction (R) would be determined by $\sqrt{F^2 + S^2}$. Because F is not constant but decreases, line R curves, a little at first because F is far stronger than S, then increasingly as F decreases and S gets proportionally stronger.

Bowls is very popular in Japan, who entered the world championships for the first time in 1980. Japanese ladies *(left)* bring special elegance to the game. *Below:* A match in progress on a Japanese hotel roof.

green in the opposite direction. Except in singles, a match consists of a stipulated number of 'ends'. In singles victory normally goes to the first player scoring 21, though in Australia and some other countries they play '31 up'.

In fours each participant delivers two bowls per end, in triples three per end and in pairs and singles four per end. Bowls are delivered alternatively, opponent by opponent, with the winner or winning unit of the previous end going first.

In fours, triples and pairs each lead (first two men) delivers his two bowls alternatively with his opposite number. In triples and fours the leads are followed by the number twos and the number twos and third men respectively. The final bowls of each end are delivered by the 'skip' – short for skipper, or rink director as he is known in Australia and some other places.

The number twos keep the score cards and the third men carry out any measuring that may be necessary when naked eyes cannot discern which of a number of bowls is nearest to the jack. The lead places the mat at the start of each end, usually at the spot of his choice but sometimes as instructed by his skip.

Originally in the history of the present day game, bowls were shaped from lignum vitae, a particularly hard wood. Though its density is such that it will sink in water, it is still lighter, volume for volume, than some plastics. Consequently, until 1962 the permitted weight of a bowl depended on its size; the bigger the bowl, the greater the volume of lignum vitae, the heavier its weight.

This weight for size rule was universally scrapped in 1980 for one which merely stipulates the maximum and minimum size and weights for bowls without attempting to relate one to the other. So composition bowls of minimum size might weigh the maximum allowed if they are fabricated from a dense plastic material.

The control that can be exercised over the density of a composition bowl gives a manufacturer scope to experiment with shape.

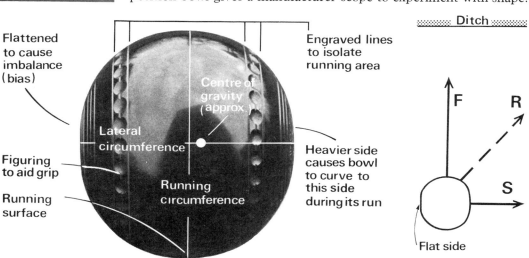

Flattened to cause imbalance (bias)

Engraved lines to isolate running area

Centre of gravity (approx.)

Lateral circumference

Figuring to aid grip

Running surface

Running circumference

Heavier side causes bowl to curve to this side during its run

Ditch

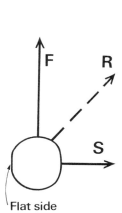

Flat side

9

Above: Umpire's Association Chairman Graham Howard examining and verifying bowls at the start of the English Championship.

Above centre: A method of finding the correct size of bowl suitable to yourself is to circle the bowl around the running circumference. When the tips of thumbs and middle fingers just meet you have an indication of the correct size of bowl, however *(above right)* the middle finger of the hand you use for bowling might well be slightly longer than the other, so you might choose a slightly larger bowl to compensate.

To-day probably 90 per cent of the bowls used in the IBB game around the world are made from plastic. This is important because the hardness and texture of a bowling green exercises a profound effect on the way any bowl performs. To compensate for this, bowls used in, say, New Zealand or Australia, where the greens are hard, generally differ somewhat from those used in Northern Britain or Canada where the climate tends to produce much softer greens.

Remember, a bowl is biassed because one side is slightly flattened, so leaving the other side slightly heavier in weight. So as it rolls towards the other end of the green the bowl will experience two forces working on it.

One is the forward force caused by the initial propulsion by its deliverer. The other is the sideways force exercised by the extra weight on one side.

Thus it will not run in a straight line but in a curve, the shape of which at any particular moment in the bowl's journey down the green will depend on the relative strengths of those two forces. The faster it is moving, the greater will be the forward force of propulsion. As it slows down the sideways force of bias will become ever stronger (see diagram 1).

Returning to greens for a moment, in IBB sanctioned championships greens must be 40 to 44 yards (36 to 40 metres) square, divided into rinks by strings running from one end to the other. The rinks must be 18 to 19 feet (5·5 to 5·8 metres) wide. The green must be surrounded by a ditch 2 to 8 inches (50 to 200 mm) below the level of the playing surface and the ditch backed by a bank not less than 9 inches (230 mm) above the level of the green, preferably upright but definitely at an angle not more than 35 degrees from the perpendicular.

A closely cut, thinly sown, sunbaked green offers far less resistance to any given bowl than one of thickly sown, uncut grass made soft and yielding by rain or continued dampness.

On the former, as frequently found in Australia, a bowl can take 16 or more seconds to come to a rest at a distance 30 yards (27·4 metres) in front of the mat from which it is delivered. In New Zealand that time can be extended to over 20 seconds.

Move to a poorly maintained green in the north-west of Britain and the same bowl may be brought to a stop at 30 yards in 9 seconds or even less.

Such greens are called 'slow' because the last part of the bowl's run ends very abruptly.

On a low resistance green the bowl trickles on and on for several seconds before stopping. In the manner of a billiards table, on which a ball will go up and down its length many times, such greens are called fast.

Remember this seeming anomaly. The quicker a bowl comes to a halt, the slower the green. The longer the bowl trickles on, the faster the green.

It is important because it affects not only the bowls you should choose but also the style of delivery you should find most advantageous.

Recalling the forces working on a bowl, it should be easy to realise that the longer it takes slowing down to a stop, the greater will be the effect of the sideways force – bias – relative to the forward force, and so the greater will be the amount of the curve of the bowl. In fact, on a 17 seconds green – that is one on which a bowl's run will take 17 seconds from start to stop 30 yards away – the last part of the curve may actually result in the bowl trickling an inch or so back towards the end from which it was delivered; in other words, a turn of 180 degrees.

Conversely, on a 10 seconds green – 10 seconds from start to stop 30 yards away – the trickle at the end of the run will be so short in time and distance that the bowl will hardly turn at all. Casting your mind back to the Duke of Suffolk and how his makeshift bowl curved round those of his opponents, you can see this is a great disadvantage.

All bowls bearing the IBB or BIBC stamp have been tested against a standard bowl kept by each authorised tester, and re-tested every 10 years. They must not have less bias than the master but they may have more. Maybe by now you can realise that choosing the right bowls to buy and use is quite a tricky operation. In fact some bowlers who compete on many greens of varying quality keep several sets of bowls from which they choose after seeing the condition of the green on which they are about to play. It is not permitted to change your bowls once a match has started. How, then, can a beginner set about choosing the set of bowls best suited to his needs?

First comes size. Delivering a bowl over 38 yards or so of flat grass so that it comes to rest on a spot the size of a 10-penny piece, or even less, demands exceptional sensitivity of touch. That sensitivity is virtually impossible if one's hand and fingers are over-stretched or clenched too tightly.

By and large, any bowler whose ambitions run a little beyond an

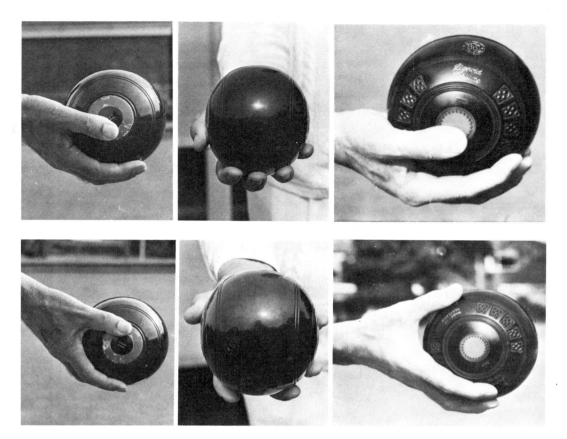

Top, left and centre: the cradle grip from side and front. The middle finger lies at the centre of the running surface, the thumb below the centre of the bowl.

Top right: The full cradle grip, with the bowl resting farther back in the palm of the hand.

Above, left and centre: The claw grip, with the thumb gripping the bowl rather than cradling it. The thumb is above the centre of the bowl and the fingers more widely spread.

Above right: The full claw grip with the thumb on top of the bowl.

evening out of doors and a yarn with a few pals on the green should choose the largest and heaviest bowl he can hold and control completely, especially through the area of his swing where he actually releases his bowl.

If he is keen to improve and can afford the cost, he should consider using two different sets, one slightly larger than the other because he will need to grip the bowl slightly harder when playing in wet or slippery conditions.

One frequently used way of finding the correct size is to form a circle with the tips of one's thumbs and middle fingers around the running circumference of the bowls under consideration. Those tips should just meet. However, it is often the case that the middle finger of the right hand is fractionally longer than the middle finger of the left hand. My own is approximately one eighth of an inch longer so that in choosing a set of bowls with that system I should probably decide on a set one eighth of an inch larger than those suggested by circling them with my middle fingers and thumbs.

Your choice should also be related to the grip you use and the delivery style you eventually adopt. For that reason, beginners and novices should try to play with borrowed bowls until their styles become regularised.

There are two fundamental ways of gripping a bowl though

12

there are many individual variations and mixtures of the two. In one the bowl sits well back in the palm and is rolled out of the hand with minimum control by the thumb. This is known as the cradle grip.

The alternative, the claw grip, has the bowl sitting nearer to the base of the fingers which, with the thumb, grip the bowl as distinct from cradling it.

The practical effects of these grips will be explained later. For the moment just take mental note that they do have differing effects on the way a bowl performs.

With size and weight decided one should next consider the material from which the bowl has been fabricated and its shape. There is a relationship between the two.

A bowl possesses two important circumferences and shapes. One is the circumference measured around the running surface of the bowl. Clearly, this must be perfectly circular if the bowl is to run smoothly over the green instead of hopping and bumping.

The other is measured around the circumference which is at right angles to the running surface. This is sometimes called the width of the bowl. Recalling the Duke of Suffolk once more, we know that one side of the bowl is flatter that the other, this causing the imbalance – bias – which causes the bowl to travel in a curve instead of straight. Because of this flattened side, the circumference of the bowl cannot be used as the running surface unless you wish to see your bowl going down the green in a series of small kangaroo leaps.

Because it is not the running surface, that sideways shape can be varied quite considerably from a pure circle with a small flat section in it. Because of the weight-size relationship which once applied in Britain, full-size lignum vitae bowls need to be as nearly spherical as possible; that is the only way there can be enough wood to reach the stipulated weight. On the other hand, because composition bowls can be of greater density, they can shed some of that side weight and still reach maximum weight. Thus many composition bowls are almost elliptical when viewed from in front or behind as they roll down the green. As with grips, I shall explain the ways differing shapes affect performance later on. For the moment, accept the generalisation that spherical bowls tend to be better on slow, heavy greens while elliptical composition bowls are superior on harder, faster greens.

Diagram 2: The varying shapes of a running surface (exaggerated) seen from in front or behind: (a) the flattened spherical shape, typical in Britain; (b) the elliptical shape common in New Zealand.

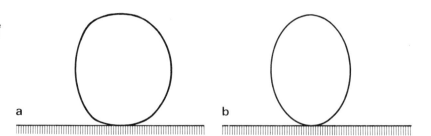

That is another reason why I seriously advise any beginner or ambitious novice to experiment with borrowed bowls for as long as possible before spending the £60 to £80 or even more needed to buy a new set to-day. Certainly delay until you have finished reading this book.

There is no need to delay in this manner before equipping oneself with suitable and correct clothing. In match play and, especially, important championships and tournaments, whites are compulsory, at least in the IBB game. It almost goes without saying that they should be well fitting, for there is considerable bending and straightening up during a game. The average singles match lasts around 80 minutes while in pairs, triples or fours 200 minutes is nearer par and some matches last over 240 minutes.

Modern man-made fabrics look smart and most have the advantage of easy washing without need of ironing. Nevertheless, I believe the breathing and absorption qualities of wool to be even more advantageous, especially in Britain, considering the vagaries of the climate with its rapid fluctuations between cold and heat, sunshine and rain.

Certainly I am convinced that every bowler should be equipped with an all-wool sweater or cardigan which he should put on immediately he feels the slightest trace of coldness. This crops up relatively often in matches started in late afternoon sunshine and finished in the late evening cool.

Socks and shoes are of paramount importance. In, say, a pairs match each player normally delivers a minimum of 84 bowls. This entails bending down to pick up a three and a half pound weight and then bending down once more to propel that weight some 30 yards across a grassy surface. Additionally, he will walk anything from one to two miles, perhaps even more if he is a compulsive chaser up the green of every bowl he delivers, during play and those 21 changes of end.

Here my recommendation for wool is particularly strong for natural fibres are undoubtedly more sympathetic to one's feet than synthetics. The socks should be well fitting, totally free of lumpy darnings and always sweetly clean. Take as much care in your selection of socks as you do over shoes.

The ideal shoe has many special features. A resiliant, light, flexible sole, which accepts the considerable bending associated with delivery without imposing unnecessary strain on the foot is best. It must be wide enough to prevent any part of the entire base of the foot overhanging it and so forcing the uppers into a supporting role.

The rules demand that the soles be flat. Maybe our ancient predecessors went around barefooted but present day human beings have become accustomed to raised heels and any sudden switch to flat footedness can set up foot and leg strain, especially to the Achilles tendon. So an interior-of-shoe heel raise is important. As a last resort, such supports can be bought at many shops but better that they are inbuilt by the manufacturer.

The back of the shoe should be of rounded design to allow more natural 'rolling' of the foot into a normal stride after delivering. This saves the heel and Achilles tendon from undue strain.

The Achilles tendon lies just below the surface at the back of the heel and it is prone to strain through excessive stretching and jarring. In bowls there is a good deal of the former and not too much of the latter. Nevertheless, your shoe should incorporate a padded leather collar for comfort and support around the ankle. It must not be so tight that it applies pressure to the Achilles tendon area when striding or stretching.

Finally, three or four hours of walking, bending and stretching under a warm sun can generate considerable foot heat and this should be dispersed. So adequate ventilation or material which 'breathes' freely is essential.

Originally the rules specified tan or black shoes but white became permissible in 1978.

Most manufacturers of bowls shoes are alert to these requirements but nothing destroys enjoyment more readily than tight, ill-fitting or overhot shoes which are hurting the feet. So watch for the features listed above when next buying bowls shoes. In fact, why limit your knowledge to the selection of bowls shoes. Apply the same principles to all shoe purchases.

By now you should have sufficient knowledge to go out on a

Above: Bowls is a game that has long been enjoyed by both sexes. This is a general view of the English Amateur National Championships at Wimbledon Park in 1961.

Above right: Players of all ages enjoy bowls, and it is never too early to learn. It is now taught in some schools.

green, perhaps in a nearby public park, and to try your hand at delivering bowls towards a jack at the far end of the rink to which you have been directed. After your first or, maybe, second try, seek out a qualified teacher who will give you a series of lessons. The secretary of your county Bowling Association should have a list of coaches in your vicinity. If you experience trouble in ascertaining his name and address, call your local Sports Council representative or visit any nearby sports centre. If that is not possible, write for help to: The Secretary, English Bowling Association, 2a Iddesleigh Road, Bournemouth, BH37JR; please enclose a self-addressed, stamped envelope for a reply.

Let me reiterate that Bowls is a challenging, skill-demanding game. It is played in more than 20 countries scattered around the world, by possibly the most courteous, friendly, hospitable brotherhood of people in the entire field of sport. You need never be lonely, no matter which bowling country you visit, once you have progressed out of the beginner-novice class.

So in playing Bowls show it the same respect you afford to, say, your parents or family. Consider yourself one of the game's ambassadors and so dress as neatly and cleanly as you would if your boss had invited you and your wife to dinner.

On or off the green, behave always with dignity and scrupulously observe the concepts of good sportsmanship. Be modest in victory and gracious when defeated. Let your conqueror enjoy to the limit his moment of triumph but whilst you are doing so, quietly analyse why you lost and he won. Resolve you will put it right next time you meet.

No matter how disappointed and upset you feel, cover it all with a smile that hides your increasing determination to improve enough to win next time. No matter how it hurts you, smile yourself into a mental state that will bring you victory next time.

Chapter Two
The Delivery: Drawing the Jack

It is now time for you to go out on a green, either to try your hand for the first time or to think about the points raised in chapter one and to discover how they can help you by trying them out.

Here let me emphasise the important part played by experiment and creativity in bringing about improvement in the game in general and players in particular. The explanation is covered by one simple sentence. It runs 'without imagination it is impossible to progress beyond what has already been done.'

You will need some bowls, a jack and a mat from which you have to deliver each bowl. It has to be placed in accordance with the laws of the game.

At the beginning of the first end of a match that position is defined in the laws 'the player to play first shall place the mat lengthwise on the centre line of the rink, the back edge of the mat to be four feet from the ditch.'

The mat's position may not be changed during any one end but at the start of the next end and all others that follow 'the mat shall not be less than four feet from the rear ditch and the front edge not less than 27 yards (25 metres) from the front ditch and on the centre line of the rink of play.'

This law has important tactical connotations because it is possible in play to find a mat position which suits you best while causing your opponent the maximum difficulty in terms of maintaining the length and direction of his deliveries.

You must have one foot actually touching or hovering in mid-air over the mat until each bowl has left your hand and is on its way down the green.

The position of the mat, although variable, is governed by the rules, and the bowler must have one foot on the mat or hovering in mid-air above it until the bowl is delivered.

In match play the winner of the toss has the right to deliver the first bowl, which means he first delivers the jack. When it comes to rest it has to be 'centred' with the pegs marking the centre of the rink and it must then be at least 25 yards (23 metres) from the front of the mat. If it is less than 25 yards or if the player delivers with such strength that it runs into the ditch, the jack is then rebowled by the other player who has the right to change the mat position if he so wishes. If, in turn, he delivers the jack short or into the ditch, it reverts to the first player but the mat automatically goes to the starting position; with its back four feet from the ditch.

There are two fundamental styles of delivery in common use. One is from an upright starting position, the bowler lowering his position so that he releases his bowl actually on the green during a

Above: John Scadgell, former Empire Games gold medallist, illustrates the athletic delivery.

Right and below: Ray Robinson uses the crouch delivery.

continuous backwards and forward swing of his arm. This is called either the upright or the athletic delivery.

The other is from a crouching position, hand at green level, before the swing begins. This is known as the crouch delivery.

Some players actually have their back knee on the ground in a type of delivery known as the full crouch.

The two types of delivery are shown in the pictures of John Scadgell, an Empire Games gold medallist and one of the great players of English bowls history, and Ray Robinson, the highly talented Lincolnshire player.

Try both methods, at first in fairly rapid succession, later at some length in turn. Each system has its inherent advantages and disadvantages but I will elaborate on these later. At the moment you should experiment. Generalising, the crouch delivery is more effective on fast greens than slow. On the latter a bowler often needs extra body momentum to deliver a bowl 30 to 35 yards without strain; that forward step in unison with the arm swing provides that extra momentum.

Apart from the inherent differences between the upright and crouching delivery positions, the way in which you use your arm creates differences in the behaviour of the bowl. So far as bowls is concerned, there are two ways of propelling the bowl down the green. One is by swinging your arm rather like a pendulum. The other is by eliminating any extensive backswing and so pushing the bowl towards the jack.

Below: Ray Robinson's delivery photographed from the side shows the restricted backswing. Compare this with that of D. Bell overleaf.

D. Bell favours the
pendulum swing. Notice
how far back the delivery
arm goes and how he uses
his body momentum to
propel the bowl forward.
Compare with Ray
Robinson's delivery on the
previous page.

The differences show clearly in the sequence pictures of D. Bell,
wearing the hat, and Ray Robinson. Apart from Robinson's
minimal backswing, he also makes little use of body momentum or
pivot as demonstrated by Bell.

Normally, 'pushers' tend to have their delivery hands more
under the bottom of their bowls at the moment of release. This
tends to apply some skid to the bowl. 'Swingers' usually have their
hands further behind the bowl and this reduces the skid, an
important factor in consistency of length.

However, another factor can introduce skidding of each bowl
you deliver. That factor is the position of your thumb during
delivery and the pressure it applies to the bowl in conjunction with
your middle finger. Look at the picture and you can see that the
thumb on top of the bowl and the middle finger below it are
squeezing it. Imagine a tense situation near the end of an important match and it is easy to understand how tension can set up
extra pressure on the bowl and so tend to squeeze it out of the
hand in addition to swinging or pushing it with the arm. This
squeezing will vary from delivery to delivery but there is one
constant feature: the skid imparted will reduce length for any
one strength of swing and also tend to launch the bowl a fraction
to the left of the intended line. The outcome is reflected by the
immense number of bowls delivered at critical stages which are
short and thin; that means they finish to the left of the desired
position.

The claw grip specifically necessitates use of the thumb but the
cradle grip aims more to roll the bowl out of the hand, as distinct
from pushing it slightly from underneath.

Study the hands of David Bryant and Alec Jackson, both great
champions by world standards, at approximately the same moment
after their bowl has left the hand. Bryant's hand and arm make
virtually a straight line and the bowl is running on the grass.
Jackson, who uses a crouch delivery and a slight pushing rather
than swinging arm action, has curled the palm up towards the sky
and the bend in his elbow indicates a further factor which has

resulted in the bowl leaving his hand above green level instead of right on it. The picture was taken during a quarter-final of the English Singles Championship of 1976. Jackson is a multi-capped international and a former winner of the English Indoor Singles Championship. He possesses a superb temperament yet even he can falter in delivery when the pressure is on. How much likelier it is that a novice or inexperienced tournament player will suffer inaccuracies through varying pressures on his bowls set up by thumb action.

So if this cause of varied deliveries is to be minimised an extra check must be made when buying a first or new set of bowls. The thumb has to come into a delivery, even when the cradle grip is used, but its effect limited so that the squeezing situation can be avoided.

The answer is to pick up the bowl you are studying and, using your normal grip, turn over your hand so that the ball is underneath. Start off by trying one of maximum diameter and then keep changing down in size, one eighth of an inch at a time. At first you will, almost certainly, feel a strain but as you continue reducing size you will arrive at a size that imposes no strain. That is the size for you. The change is quite sudden. One size causes strain, the next one does not.

As an extra precaution, study the back part of your arm just above the wrist. Strain will show itself through corrugations on the back of the arm. When there is no strain the back of the arm is smoother. The pictures show this point.

Above left: David Bryant's arm in delivery is straight. Note the palm of the hand turned inwards by 45°.

Above: Alec Jackson's delivery is quite different to Bryant's. The arm is bent and the palm of the hand faces the sky.

To reduce squeezing set up by thumb action, test that the bowl is of a correct size by holding the bowl in your normal grip and inverting it, as shown in the illustrations. The corrugations standing out on the back of the arm *(left)* show strain, whereas with the slightly smaller bowl the smooth back of the forearm *(right)* shows there is no strain.

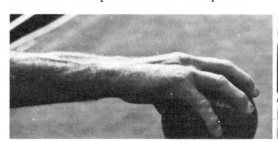

The actual shape of the bowl along its running axis – its width – should also be considered. The shape of the bowl should conform with the shape of your palm and so fill it comfortably. Some men may find that a spherical bowl fills the hand comfortably while an elliptical one does not, and vice versa. However, shape affects the way a bowl performs so a little compromise may be necessary.

Finally, weight. Simply choose the heaviest you can manage comfortably.

All these factors exercise differing effects in wet or dry weather. On a hot, sunny day the bowl remains dry and providing your hand does not sweat too freely, your grip on even an over-size bowl will feel secure. Come a wet, cold day and you may find the bowl slipping. You will normally try to counter this through additional of your thumb. However, wet and cold usually means a slower green which is less sensitive to the refinements of good touch than a dry, fast green. So the varying pressure exercised by your thumb will not matter so much. In general, then, study the points about bowls selection in this and the preceding chapter and then buy the largest bowls you can handle and deliver comfortably.

Bowls can be obtained with many patterns of figuring to aid grip. Bowler's views on how much is necessary vary, and it is very much a personal choice.

Whether or not the bowls you choose should be adorned with fancy figuring around the side, as shown in the picture, depends on how much grip you need to apply with your thumb. Some bowlers would rate the grip-aiding figuring shown to be inadequate, others the reverse. Generalising, one's finger tips are among the most sensitive parts of a human being and that sensitivity should be inflicted with as little excessive stimulation as is consistent with control and accuracy.

The shape of the bowl across its running surface affects the way it runs. A spherical bowl distributes weight across a bigger radius than one which is more elliptical. On soft greens, therefore, the spherical bowl will remain more on the surface while the elliptical shaped bowl will sink in a fraction and thus suffer the braking effect on its side that one can see applied by the brakes on a bicycle. Thus the sphere will take more time trickling to a stop than the ellipse, so giving the bias extra time in which the bowl will turn.

Conversely, on hard greens which offer far less resistance that extra time taken in coming to a stop imposes considerable pressure on a bowler's control and consistency: indeed, on a very fast green such control can be completely negated by a strongish wind, since the bowl's 'braking system' will be less than the wind's powers of propulsion, so much so that in New Zealand it can stop, only to be moved once more by a puff of wind. Under such conditions the elliptical bowl enjoys superior control because of its inbuilt 'brakes'. This restricts the extent of its turn during the final stages of its journey down the green.

The practical effect is that the vast majority of bowls to-day are made from synthetic material while the minority of lignum vitae woods are sold in the northern areas of Britain. Now even those sales are diminishing because English manufacturers of 'compositions' are using a slightly less dense 'mix' and so turning out bowls nearer to a spherical shape on the running surface.

All this may seem intensely scientific and I am the last person to negate that idea. Certainly read the material carefully and thoughtfully but realise it is a guide rather than a command. The bowls you eventually buy and use will be your 'tools'. Thus your feelings about them are more important than anything else. Be guided, certainly, but do not allow yourself to be brain-washed.

Reiterating that the object of the game is to position one's bowls nearer to the jack than those of the opposition, it follows that, all other things being equal, the player with the technically best and smoothest flowing method of sending his bowl down the green – the best delivery – should win. This in no way negates the importance of tactical and temperamental ability and the intangibles of character. Nor indeed, does it minimise the part that luck, good and bad, can have on the outcome of a match. That is recognised in my words 'all other things being equal'.

In the coaching of world class tennis champions I evolved the concept 'competitive success derives from confidence and confidence is the child of competence.' I call it the 'three Cs' formula. Dynamic bowls competence is centred on a sound method of delivery, a wide range of shots, and the knowledge of how to exploit those qualities i.e. sound strategical and tactical knowledge.

The basic qualities can be developed on the green – and to some degree, off it – through intelligent study, practice and determination. Improvement of the intangibles can also be achieved but through somewhat different techniques. They come in later chapters. First learn the fundamentals of a good delivery.

Two physical factors come into the reckoning here. One is a good body balance, the other is freedom of total movement. If one cannot maintain unwavering balance there can be no chance of consistency of swing and, therefore, accuracy and consistency. And

if one suffers from muscular restrictions or is subject to pain in the
joints, then balance must be affected. Because many bowlers have
played other games when young, a lot suffer from osteo-arthritis;
fair wear and tear of the joints is a reasonable description of that
situation.

Jack Nicklaus says graphically 'you hit a golf ball with your legs'
and this theory is, in some ways, applicable to bowls. If all your
foot and leg joints plus those of your hips and waist are strong,
supple and pain-free you are enjoying something of a bonus so far
as your bowls delivery is concerned. It means you should be able
to adopt the athletic (upright) delivery. By and large this is somewhat superior to the crouch in British conditions.

Stanley Lant, winner with Bob Keenlyside of the 1978 English
Bowling Association Pairs Championship at the age of 32, is a
typical and effective exponent of this type of delivery. The pictures
and description show in some detail his full delivery.

Notice how he adjusts his body and stance while using his right
arm to help 'sight' the line along which he wishes to project his
bowl. His feet form a 'V' and the swing of his arm virtually bisects
that 'V'. Specifically, his left foot is pointing slightly wide of the
line of his delivery. This is an important detail for it ensures that
the latter part of his arm swing does not travel across the line set
up by his front foot and leading (left) leg. Swinging across this
imaginary line is detrimental to good balance.

Many bowlers use the right foot as a guide to the intended line
of delivery. This many find helpful but its positive goodness is less
significant than the definite badness of bowling across one's leading
leg.

Note, too, how his left arm tucks slightly across his body. Many
bowlers place their left hands on the upper part of their left legs to
help security and regularity. This it does do, but at the expense of
a certain amount of body pivot. Lant's pivot brings his right
shoulder into action during the release area, so adding a little

forward momentum to his overall delivery. This swing increases his power somewhat and so enables him to obtain length with less apparent physical strength than bowlers who limit this pivot by anchoring their left side in planting the left hand on the left leg. This lessening of the need to 'power' the bowl helps smoothness but on a day when one's confidence or feeling of rhythm is below par it can lead to inaccuracy and diminished consistency.

Lant makes good use of his head, first keeping it steady until after the moment of release and then turning it smoothly downwards and slightly forwards. This minimises the likelihood of the upwards jerking swing that is the commonest fault in any ball game, bowls included.

The forward movement is in keeping with the Alexander system, which is virtually standard teaching in an activity in which meticulous balance is even more important than in bowls, ballet dancing.

Lant has maintained body balance by letting his right leg swing forward in a running movement and by touching the green with his outstretched right hand.

Maybe one might look for an arm swing nearer to a true pendulum but the general freedom and rhythm of the delivery maybe provides some visual evidence of his consistency in drawing bowls to the jack, an important factor in winning that pairs championship.

Drawing to the jack? What does it mean? The term is almost self-explanatory. It is the shot in which the delivered bowl draws in closely to the jack. It is the most important shot in the game. Develop your ability to deliver bowl after bowl within two or three inches of the jack, irrespective of its length from the mat or the strains and stresses of the match situation, and you will win nine matches for every one you lose.

Tony Higgs, the young Hertfordshire international illustrated, is another exponent of the upright delivery though his body weight is forward momentarily earlier than Lant's while his left arm stays clear of his body, so giving considerable freedom of movement. His use of it in conjunction with his right leg helps him maintain good balance throughout his delivery.

Tony Higgs uses the upright delivery but lets his left arm swing freely instead of locking it by holding his left leg.

Malcolm Henderson grips his left upper leg with his left hand. This stabilizes his delivery position, and helps to lock his left foot to the ground when following through.

On the other hand, Malcolm Henderson of Northumberland uses the left hand on leg method. In the picture his left foot is flat on the green during the follow through, in contrast to the lift displayed by Lant.

These differences are more significant in written words than they are on the green itself, if only because each of those bowlers possesses other factors which compensate. However, great oaks from little acorns grow and if my 'three Cs formula' has any meaning for you, those tiny details are 'acorns'.

Whichever variation of these is used, the need for good balance during the swing remains imperative. This balance owes much to leg strength and control. Sadly, as one grows older there is a natural tendency for those qualities to deteriorate. This deterioration can be minimised, perhaps even halted, by a sound systematic and sustained daily programme of suitable exercises. Human beings being what they are, only strongly motivated enthusiasts are likely to maintain such a regimen. David Bryant, the world champion and holder of the Commonwealth Games singles title from 1972 through until the 1980s, and former British Isles Indoor Champion, Alan Windsor, are two ambitious players who train diligently when preparing for important events. Older, less ambitious people may not think that such self discipline and, perhaps, sacrifice is for them. If they are not naturally supple or do not exercise in other ways, say brisk walking or even jogging, they sometimes adopt a delivery style based on balancing the body first and then swinging their arms in projecting their bowls – the crouch delivery.

Indeed, on fast greens (14 seconds upwards. Check back to chapter one to ensure you understand about fast and slow greens) on fast greens less power is needed to propel a bowl 38 yards (35 metres) than is the case on slow, heavy surfaces. Thus the loss of body momentum may not matter; the pendulum action of the arm can be sufficient . . . and without any need for accuracy endangering 'muscling'.

Because of this one rarely sees crouch delivery bowlers who

excel in the firing shot, or drive, as it is known in Australia and America. As its name suggests, the drive is a destructive weapon 95 per cent of the times it is used. The disposition of bowls around the jack – the 'head' – is unfavourable and the best answer appears to be a complete scattering by a bowl crashing into the middle of them.

Maybe a crouch delivery can develop sufficient power without undue loss of accuracy on a fast green but when that green slows down to, say, 10 seconds the necessary use of muscular power handicaps accuracy alarmingly.

So the style you adopt is likely to be conditioned by your ambitions and the geographical situation of the place where you bowl most frequently. It is also affected by your basic personality. Bold, aggressive extroverts tend to turn more easily to forceful tactics than more thoughtful introverts. The former usually adopt the athletic upright delivery while the players who rely more on finesse than force often find a crouch delivery better suited to their exploitation of touch sensitivity.

Take care that you do not misinterpret the difference between the upright and crouch deliveries. Ray Robinson stands upright while surveying the head and then lowers his body while taking his delivery arm back. Then he halts the continuity of the delivery by touching the ground with his bowl at the point where he will release it. Finally, he then delivers his bowl as almost a separate operation.

Ray Robinson's delivery. Though he starts from an upright position he moves into a crouch before actual delivery.

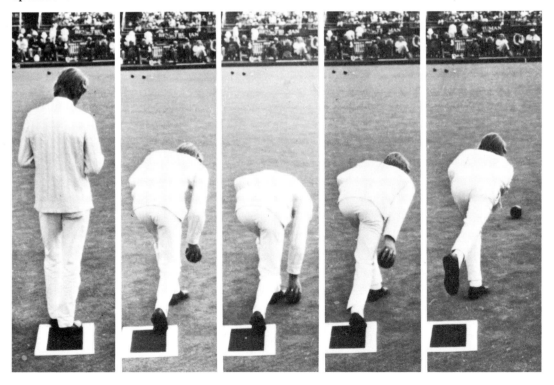

He is tall, lithe and with a longish arm. His use of a pendulum swing, as distinct from a push, added to his physical assets, minimise any disadvantages of delivering from a fixed position.

Shorter, plumper, less athletic players lack these natural attributes but they are to be even more handicapped in terms of the upright delivery. So they can find the crouch delivery the better.

The arm swing should follow as straight a line as possible along the one taken when the bowl is released. Eventually, the arm has to curve away across the front of the body. This straightness of swing is ably demonstrated by the pictures taken from behind Robinson. A similar study of David Bryant's delivery shows a similarly straight to and fro swing with no hint of the arm twisting slightly behind his back at the end of the backswing, a common fault seen all too often on club and parks greens.

Though he starts from a crouch position, David Bryant's swing is continuous from the moment he straightens up to completion of follow-through.

Bryant reduces arm strain by turning his hand so that the bowl is uppermost at the end of his backswing, a technique which was also used by Arthur Knowling, a brilliant international of the 1950s. By turning his hand through 180 degrees he is able to extend his backswing without feeling any strain along the back of his forearm and hand or above the elbow. In reducing strain he lessens the danger it brings of variations of length and direction.

One further, fine point emerges from the pictures, namely the aligning of the hands. Stand up a moment and let your arm hand straight down at the side of your body. Then turn your wrist so that the palm of your hand is facing forwards. You will probably feel some strain in the area of your elbow. Furthermore, if your elbow is touching your body, the lower part of your arm will angle slightly away from your upper leg; the arm does not form a straight line.

Next turn your palm inwards by some 45 degrees. The strain disappears and, additionally, the arm now makes a straight line.

Look at the last picture in the Robinson sequence and you will see that the palm of his hand is facing straight up the green. Now turn to the equivalent picture in the Bryant sequence and it can be seen that his hand is angled inwards by that strain-reducing 45 degrees.

The majority of bowlers favour the palm forwards style, claiming that constant use of it eliminates the strain. As an advantage, they point out that the middle finger can then be placed precisely in the middle of the running surface, so avoiding tilting the bias away from its maximum position and so helping consistency of line and turn.

In turning his hand inwards Bryant cannot place his middle finger in that central position. Instead, it has to be above the maximum position and this removes the easy way of keeping the bowl on its keel end after end.

In fact Bryant seemingly finds no difficulty in maintaining a constant position for his grip. On the face of things, turning the hand slightly inwards does introduce a variable missing with the palm forwards delivery. Whether the simplicity of the palm forwards compensates for the slightly reduced strain of the palm turned grip is something each bowler must decide for himself. Keeping the palm studiously forward does help to reduce hooking the arm across the body during the follow through so this may prove the vital factor in arriving at a decision.

A bowl's maximum curve comes when the bias is fully to the side of the bowl. By holding the bowl in a tilted position the bias can be moved nearer to the centre of the bowl. This causes it to travel in a straighter line and this can sometimes be significantly advantageous. It needs considerable skill to achieve success with this technique though it is somewhat easier when one is using lignum vitae, spherical, bowls than it is with those which are more elliptical in shape.

I cannot think of one class player who advises tilting but Percy Baker, four times English Singles champion, often used the tilt technique on fast greens when his bowls were curving excessively. The tilt showed through the distinguishing disc on the side of his bowl. With no tilt this revolves on the cross axis of the bowl and is as steady as an unblinking eye. In the picture one can see that it will be turning around that axis like the earth around the sun.

It is an advanced, risky technique. Better try adjusting your position on the mat to modify the curve of your bowl's journey.

Even if you get every bowl away absolutely centred on its running surface you may still find variations in the curve it takes which are the results of differences in your delivery, specifically in the ways your bowls leave your hand. Ideally, the speed at which the bowl rotates when leaving your hand should exactly match the speed of its forward travel on the green. That way you are neither imparting skid caused by back spin nor over-running resulting from too much overspin. Skid is more prevalent, often through over pressure by the thumb. Bearing in mind that your finger tips are among your most sensitive senses, your bowl should ideally roll from your hand to the green in the order palm, lower part of fingers, finger tips. To help this your front knee must be flexible and bent low.

This suggests the cradle grip but in the claw grip the bowl is partially carried by your finger tips. The danger lies in variations of pressure. If you are alert to this or are so relaxed in play that cum hell or high-water,your grip never varies, the claw is best for you.

Dick Bernard, silver medallist in the 1972 World Singles Championship, cradles his bowl effectively and with just the right modicum of the thumb.

A few bowlers use their fingers to impart spin or to produce slight changes of length. Two words cover my recommendation – 'forget it.' A five-inch (127 mm) diameter bowl rotates around 80 times travelling the green to a jack 100 feet (30·5 metres) from the mat. Many ends in singles – or any form of the game – are won by a bowl which is only an inch (25 mm) from the jack after the player's earlier bowl three inches (75 mm) from the jack had been bettered by one from his opponent finishing two inches (50 mm) from the jack.

The circumference of that five inch (127 mm) bowl is 15·71 inches (400 mm). This shows that changing length by a couple of inches or so of the circumference after the bowl has rotated completely some 80 times is a monumental task demanding near miracles from the man who delivers it.

Better by far that one strives for an almost automatic delivery of identical strength each time and then tries for those one inch variations by slight movements of position on the mat.

This accuracy is dependent on releasing the bowl precisely on the surface, not in pushing down on the green or letting the bowl go an inch or so in mid-air.

Apart from these mechanical considerations one faces two other problems: finding the correct line for your bowl and the length demanded by the rest of the head. Both are strongly influenced by the pace and texture of the rink on which you are bowling, Recapping quickly, the faster the green the more a bowl curves and the lesser the strength needed to propel it to any given length.

Finding direction is somewhat easier than bowling consistently to an exact length. No matter the distance of the jack from the front of the mat, the angle of delivery necessary to curl your bowl back to the centre of the rink remains the same. I am indebted to that eminent American mathematician and player, Parker Allen, for the table which gives the breakdown of time needed for a bowl to home on to a jack situated at varying lengths on the same green.

The farther the distance of the jack, the longer the time of the 'trickle' of the bowl but as it goes farther out from the centre line before starting to bend, that angle of delivery remains steady. In fact as no bowling green can be perfectly paced and true over its

Dick Barnard's grip.

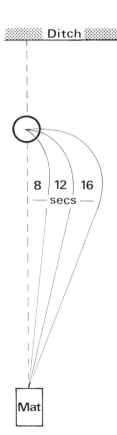

Diagram 3: Differences in the curve of the same bowl on greens of different pace.

Comparison of initial velocities with stopping times

Initial velocity feet per second	Time to 75 feet in secs	Time from 75 feet to stop	Distance of stop from mat in feet	Total time
13.693	10.954	—	75	10.954
13.965	9.000	2.172	78	11.172
14.230	8.332	3.052	81	11.384
14.492	7.817	3.777	84	11.594
14.748	7.445	4.353	87	11.798
15.000	7.111	4.889	90	12.000
15.248	6.844	5.334	93	12.178
15.492	6.618	5.776	96	12.394
15.732	6.408	6.178	99	12.586
15.970	6.214	6.562	102	12.776
16.200	6.037	6.923	105	12.960
16.432	5.886	7.260	108	13.146

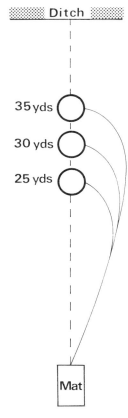

Diagram 4: The line of delivery is consistent for all lengths.

entire area – the treading of feet at its ends is one cause of variations – there will be minor adjustments of that angle, but for all practical purposes the angle of delivery is a constant. However, achieving that angle – finding the correct line for your delivery – can present even high ranking bowlers with problems. Ideally, one's instinct for the pace and other factors of the green should simplify this problem. In play something more concrete is generally sought after as an aid to confidence and, consequently, better judgement of 'land', the term usually adopted when discussing the line of a bowl to the jack.

Some bowlers seek fixtures on the banks: the position of a permanent scoreboard, a thin tree trunk, maybe the line dividing the rink from the one adjoining it. Care must be taken not to select a 'fixture' which can turn out to be the reverse; a spectator for example.

Whether or not you opt for such targets, it should be a routine exercise for you to discover by investigation exactly how wide a sweep is necessary for your bowl to curve back on to the centre of a rink at all lengths from 75 to 114 feet (23 to 35 metres) and on all greens covering the time spectrum 9 to 16 seconds. With that knowledge safely stored in mind or, better, logged on a card which can be carried at all times when playing, you can measure the width of any rink on which you play, and measure its pace on the day you play. Then you can look at your card to find that, say, you will need six feet (1·8 metres) of 'land' for your bowl to curve back to the centre of the rink. Knowing that the rink is running at, say, 14 seconds for a jack 30 yards (27·4 metres) away and that the rink is 18 feet (5·5 metres) wide, the widest part of your delivery must be three feet (0·9 metres) inside the string marking the side boundary of your rink. It is not recommended that before each shot you study your card – its purpose is to help with early deliveries.

Minor adjustments may well be necessary to compensate for variations of one kind or another on that rink. The advantage is that intelligent practice should enable you to be able to judge within an inch (25 mm) or so a whole range of distances between 24 and 108 inches (600 and 2,700 mm).

Learning to read greens in this manner should also help to develop your instinctive feeling for the angles which can be successfully exploited by a good class, thinking bowler.

Having established the line along which you wish to deliver your bowl, make use of your feet in seeking to find it. I have already revealed the danger of inconsistency brought about by pointing your left foot inwards so that your follow through runs across the line it is showing. A more positive use can be made. You are right handed. You have decided to bowl on the forehand; that is the line running away from you to the right of the jack. Select the correct line and point your foot along it. Then point your left foot at the jack. There you have the angle for your delivery. Providing you have developed a swing which is in line with your guiding foot, you should never stray far from it, especially through the wobbly balance set up by bowling across your left foot.

Switch to the backhand; the line to the left of the jack as you look down the green. This time point your left foot along the intended line of your delivery and point your right foot at the jack. Again, your feet outline the estimated angle and the left foot acts as your guide or 'sight'.

Thanks to the teachings of that fine Australian thinker, writer and player, R.T. 'Dick' Harrison, this system is widely used in that country, with effects which can be measured by the many Australian successes in the bowls world competitive scene.

Let me reiterate. A flowing, rhythmic, well-balanced delivery lays a sound foundation for accuracy and consistency. To summarise the factors which help this: (1) choice of bowls suitable in weight, size and shape for your hand; (2) adoption of a comfortable, unstressed grip: (3) good balance and suppleness; (4) a smooth, rhythmic, straight arm swing; (5) good 'grassing' of each bowl right on the surface of the green; (6) steadiness of shoulders, head and eyes through and after the release zone of the delivery; (7) sensitivity of touch; (8) smooth, unchecked follow-through; (9) accurate aligning of the feet; (10) controlled muscular relaxation throughout the entire delivery.

The average time taken between analysis of the head from the mat and the moment of release depends on the individual and varies from three seconds or so up to 11 seconds or even more, with six seconds as an optimum time interval. Too hurried a delivery brings the penalities of carelessness. Too long on the mat creates performance-destroying tension. Each bowler must discover his best timing procedure and then stick rigidly to it.

Chapter Three
The Other Shots

Unquestionably, the draw to the jack remains the primary shot of the game. Any player capable of delivering 50 per cent of his bowls within six inches (152 mm) of the jack is extremely difficult to beat, no matter who his opponent may be.

Nevertheless, it is not the only shot, and anyone seeking success in competitive circles should take care in developing those other shots which form a major battery. They are, in no special order:

1 The 'cannon' or 'wick'
2 The promotional bowl
3 The jack-trailer
4 The wrest-out (take out)
5 The drive – 'firing shot' in British terms
6 The block

When practising, the majority of players concentrate on drawing to the jack. They take their sets of four bowls and a jack on the green, deliver the jack from one end and then try to put all their bowls right on to it. Then they will repeat the exercise in the opposite direction.

Almost certainly, they will vary the length of the jack, sometimes sending it the minimum 25 yards (23 metres), at others the full 38 yards (35 metres), with all other lengths between.

This practise is important and valuable but it varies in one major way from a match. There will only be three bowls round the jack when the practicising player delivers his fourth and last bowl. In match singles there will be six or seven, in pairs and fours there can be 15 and in triples 17. Seldom is there an unobstructed path to the jack.

Consequently, bowlers are constantly facing alternatives. The head may be 'impossible' so the choice can lie between a drive which crashes the jack out of bounds for a replayed end or a highly skilful 'cannon' which results in the bowl glancing into second or third position off the target bowl.

In the former case brute force may save the position completely but failure will present the opposition with a large score. The softer alternative is extremely unlikely to prevent an adverse score but it stands a good chance of holding the opposition to, say, a two or three, may be even a single.

With the opponents three ahead and holding another three on the 21st end reducing these down to a single is useless. They've won, so what matters the score? There is no reasonable alternative to an attempt to scatter the head with a drive, so forcing the end to begin all over again.

However, such a simple choice seldom presents itself. One is forced to choose between two or more dubious alternatives. First, then, one must fully understand how two bowls behave when one cannons into the other.

Diagram 5: When the delivered bowl D hits target bowl T plumb in the centre both bowls start off along straight line S.

Diagram 6: When the delivered bowl D hits target bowl T 'half ball', the two bowls start off at around 45° from the line of delivery.

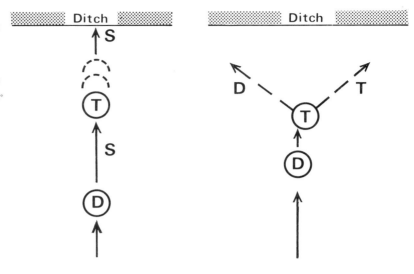

If bowl D hits the target T plumb in the middle both bowls will start off along the straight line 'S' before the bias of each takes effect (see diagram 5).

Diagram 7: When the delivered bowl D hits target bowl T nearer the edge, T starts off at a sharp angle while D proceeds nearer to its original course.

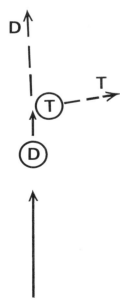

If D hits T 'half ball' (mid-way between its centre and outside edge) T will go right at an angle around 45 degrees and D will be deflected left at a similar angle. The exact angles are governed by the shapes, sizes and basic materials of the bowls (see diagram 6).

If D hits T 'thinner' (nearer the edge) than 'half ball' T will be deflected sharper to the right while D will remain nearer to its original course and speed than with the full ball or 'half ball' cannon (see diagram 7).

Remember, however, that D (the delivered bowl) will be running in a curve at the moment of impact. How big a curve (relative to a straight line down the green) is dependent on pace; the faster the delivery, the straighter the line and also the farther the two bowls will travel after impact.

The cannon makes possible some intriguing and spectacular shots, especially on fast greens – 16 or more seconds from start to stop 30 yards (27·4 metres) from the front of the mat.

I recall an example from the inaugural world championships at Kyeemagh when the South African 'wizard' Snowy Walker faced a seemingly impossible situation.

His opponent lay one, perhaps two shots, on the front of the jack which seemed well covered, both in front and at the sides, However, the green was fast and this was accentuated in the direction Walker had to bowl by a stiffish breeze.

So he chose to attempt a little cannon off bowl W1 in the diagram, relying on the pace of the green to keep his bowl trickling slower and slower until the bias actually had it moving back towards Walker for the last inch or so of its run.

The result is shown in diagram 8.

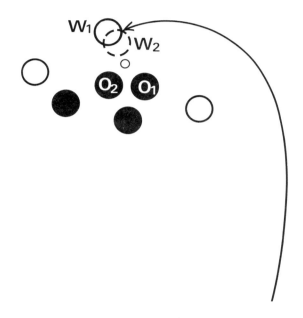

Diagram 8: The bowl (W_2) delivered by Snowy Walker which moved back towards Walker to drop off W_1 and give him the shot.

His bowl, W2, dropped straight back off W1 to the jack to give Walker a very valuable one. Such a shot would have been impossible on a slow green.

There is no way in which this or any book can legislate for every eventuality. The facts about angles taken after a cannon are fundamentally correct. How your bowls relate to those of other players is something you must discover from practice and play. So when you go out on the green alone, take a few bowls other than your own and then try cannoning off them to learn the angles and distances after contact taken by the two bowls – yours and the target – at varying speeds.

Always bear in mind the line your bowl should be travelling at the moment of impact. Remember that on a slow green it might deviate only 10 degrees from the straight line whilst on a fast green it can be almost 180 degrees. However, at 180 degrees your bowl would be moving so slowly that it could not move a target bowl, or cannon off it, more than an inch.

The promotional shot is similar in concept but as it is the target bowl and not the one just delivered which has to be moved, the tactic is usually reserved for situations in which the target bowl is in front of the jack; the length of the target bowl from the mat will be less than that of the jack; it will have to be pushed forward.

A classic example of this was provided by several times Welsh champion Tom Yeoman in his final against Reg Baker when Baker, leading 19-18, was holding the two shots which would give him the title. Diagram 9 shows the overall position seen by Yeoman when he stepped on the mat to deliver his last bowl of the end.

There seemed no way of profiting from a forcing shot so he elected for an ambitious promotional play to 'spring' the jack on to Y1 about 18 inches away. Judging the pace and direction perfectly, he added just sufficient pace to push B2 on to B1 which in turn, pushed the jack sideways to Y1 for a match saving single (see diagram 10). A two on the next end earned Yeoman the championship.

That was a superb effort, but usually the situation is somewhat less complicated. The basic operation is to select a suitably positioned but non-scoring bowl and then to deliver another bowl which pushes it through to the jack to rob the opposition of a score.

Diagram 9: The position seen by Tom Yeoman when about to deliver his last bowl in the Welsh championship. Baker (B) held two shots.

Diagram 10: The path of Yeoman's bowl (Y₄) which hit B₂, thus pushing the jack on to Y₁ and giving Yeoman the shot.

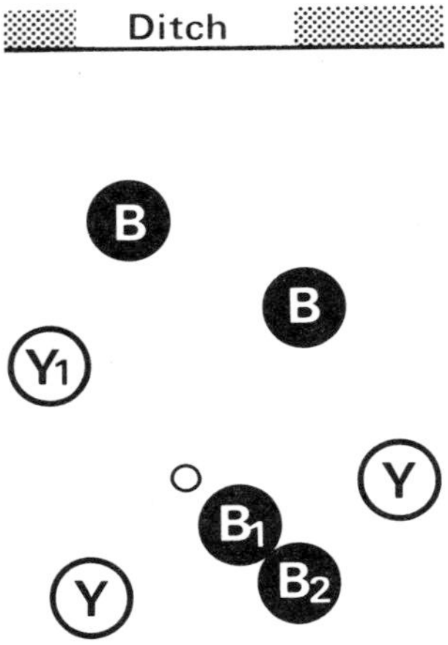

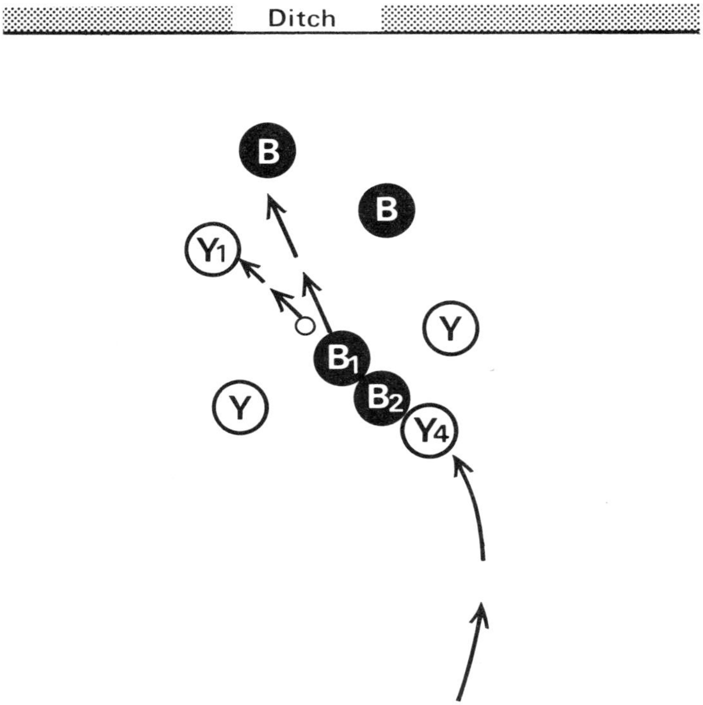

The jack-trailer is from the same stable. The opposition holds a scoring position at the head but there is a path to the jack and a promising cache of one's own bowls between the jack and the ditch.

In this one normally wishes for one's bowl to hit the jack into those back bowls and also follow along the same line in order to add another shot to the score for the end.

This entails imparting very slight top spin to the bowl at the moment of release. In reality one can seldom, if ever, impart actual top spin; the bowl is revolving slightly faster than the speed needed for the pace at which it is travelling on the green. The bowl is 'skating' slightly, perhaps through finger tip action.

It is far easier to slide one's hand under the bowl at the moment of release, so causing it to skid. Top spin, as distinct from skid, sets up a somewhat longer and more gradual a curve than skid. With this the bowl runs straighter for a longer distance, with the curving section taking a more hook-like curve.

In play the differences are comparatively tiny but the distinguishing mark of a class player, as distinct from an average participant, is his ability to change a bowl's length an inch here or its curve half an inch there.

Diagrams 11 and 12 show two situations, one in which the bowler can 'trail the jack' into a group of bowls, the other in which he needs to remove an opposition bowl without his own bowl

Diagram 11: The deliverer can convert four shots against to four shots for himself by running the jack and his own fourth ball into the nest of his own bowls (D) near the ditch, a classic jack-trailing situation.

Diagram 12: The opposition bowl (O_1) is preventing the deliverer's three bowls (D) from scoring but O_1 is there to be taken out. The deliverer will need to impart slightly more power than for a similar 'jack trailer' and he will want his bowl to stay put after hitting O_1. Because of the extra power the curve will not be so wide. Delivery with slight underspin will help him to make the bowl stop sufficiently sharply to 'stay in the count'.

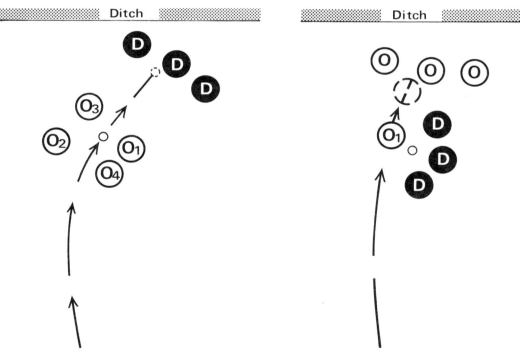

running on after impact. His own bowl stops near the jack, to secure another point.

This type of **wrest out** or take out, and also jack trailers, are valuable and imperatively necessary to any bowler with ambitions for competitive success. They are valuable both in their own rights and in the uncertainty they can and do set up in many opponents. In executing them it is necessary to relate the 'weight' of the delivery to the curve the bowl will take. Remember that the longer the bowl trickles on, the farther it will deviate from a straight line down the green. Take another look at the Snowy Walker example on page 35 and then compare it with diagram 12.

Practice is vital – and on a variety of different paced greens in order to experience the infinite variety of angles that can evolve from different paced greens and shots, to say nothing of varying types of bowls.

In general, the faster the delivery, the straighter the path of your bowl. The amount of curve of any bowls delivered with the same strengths is proportional to the pace of the green. The faster the green, the greater the curve.

The drive (firing shot) is normally a destructive weapon. Its pace is such that the bowl's forward momentum almost cancels out the sideways pull of the bowl's bias. Almost, but not quite. The bias must have some effect. On a green timed at 14 seconds the bowl will deviate by about its own width during a 30 yard (27·4 metres) run. On a 10 seconds green it may be three times that amount. Understand that these are only guides. They must not be taken completely literally, and practice with your own bowls is the only way to discover how much deviation to allow.

The block is a bowl delivered to a position on the green smack in the path the opposition wishes to use for a delivery. Considering the variety of slightly different paths open to a bowler skilled in changing his positions on the mat, this has to be a psychological weapon rather than a physical obstruction.

If the obvious path for the opposition lies on the forehand, it is best to seek the blocking position with a delivery that follows a backhand course, and vice versa if the opponent's best path is on the backhand (see diagram 13).

Clearly, no bowl should ever be wasted so every care must be taken during delivery; this is particularly true when trying to block the opponent's path. Some experts say it is impossible to achieve the objective. By inference, then, any blocking bowl is a wasted shot. Those who disagree, however, accept that a block shot has to be perfectly positioned if it is to be effective. Care, plus bowling on the opposite hand to the one best suited to the opponent, is the safest way of delivering one's bowl to the most troublesome position.

Those, then, form the main armoury of a top class player. How many of the shots he may have to use depends to a large degree on the position in the team he will be taking. In singles he will need them all. As a lead in triples or fours he can become a major contributor to winning without ever deviating from drawing to the jack. Other positions call for varying use of, perhaps, every shot there is, so the necessities for performing well in them should now be studied.

Ditch

Mat

Diagram 13: When the opponent's best path to the jack is on the forehand, as shown by the continuous line, the best path to seek when playing the blocking shot is to the backhand, as shown by the broken line, and vice versa.

Chapter Four
Positions in the Team

Attendances at the annual English Association Championships at Worthing tell without question that singles, the man against man clash, are far and away the most compelling crowd pullers.

Study the entries for the four individual events in those championships – singles, pairs, triples, fours – and you will discover that far more players are involved in events other than singles. A check of figures showed the following participant player totals: singles 12,427; pairs 23,776; triples 21,993; fours 19,840.

In club play the ratio of fours players probably increases to put it at the top of the league. Space utilisation is one reason for this. On a 40-yard (36-metre) long rink which is six yards (5·5 metres) wide the space per player figure is 30 square yards (25 square metres) per man against 120 square yards (100 square metres) per man in singles.

This is a socially important figure, especially on municipal greens for which local councils have sometimes to provide justification.

So it is essential that any bowler who is eager to improve learns to be effective in any of four positions he may be asked to fill. They are: lead, number two, third man and skip. As a first task he should familiarise himself with the special, non-bowling duties attached to each position. They are:

The Lead

The lead tosses a coin with the opposing lead to decide which of them 'has the mat' (bowls first) on the first end. In some club matches the home captain will, as a courteous gesture, hand the jack to the visiting four.

The lead who bowls first on this or any other end must lay the mat before delivering the jack. On the opening end the position is

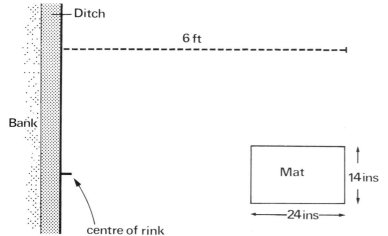

Ditch

6 ft

Bank

Mat

14 ins

24 ins

centre of rink

Diagram 14: The position for the mat on the opening end of a match. The rules state the front of the mat must be exactly six feet from the front of the ditch and in the centre of the rink.

specified by the rules; the front of the mat must be exactly six feet from the front of the ditch and on the centre of the rink (see diagram 14).

On all subsequent ends the lead in possession of the jack (winner of the previous end) may place the back of the mat not less than four feet (1·22 metres) from the ditch or anywhere else along the centre line so long as the front of the mat is not less than 27 yards (25 metres) from the front ditch. After bowling the jack he must ensure that it is 'centred' on the rink by the skip via hand signals from the mat.

Number Two

At the completion of each end the opposing number twos must enter the score on their cards, checking with one another to ensure that their cards agree. The number two must see that all names (and initials, please) are recorded on the cards.

Third Man

He is second in command to the skip and in an emergency takes over his duties. It is his special duty to measure the distance of bowls from the jack to determine the 'count' at the conclusion of each and to agree that count with his opposite number.

He also signals clearly to his skip and the number two the 'count' from the end.

The Skip

Number four in the bowling order, the skip is in total control of his team. He should seek to resolve all disputes with his opposing skips. If a dispute cannot be resolved, he must call for the umpire. He may at any time delegate his duties to another member of his team providing he notifies the opposing skip of the delegation.

If not a duty, it is an obligation that there is no ambiguity about the verbal or visual instructions he gives to his team.

All Players

Those not in the act of bowling or controlling the play must stand behind the jack and away from the head or, at the bowling end, one yard (at least) behind the mat.

This is the most disregarded rule in the full 73 listed in the official handbook of the EBA. In Australia and South Africa bowlers not actively engaged at the moment must retire to the banks of the green.

Those duties are supplemented by one which is unwritten but which should be a point of honour for all players. It is to be as soundly prepared and practised, physically and mentally, as possible; this covers appearance.

Only if that last, unwritten duty is observed can a player be ready to give of his best in the game being played. What is the best each can give? What governs the tactics each man may apply? What shots will he need? This, perhaps, is where the full fascination of the game lies.

The Lead

At this moment recall the object of the game. It is to deliver bowls nearer to the jack than those of the opposition so that at the finish of the match your total shots scored exceed those of the opposition.

It is important to keep this fully in mind. There are occasions when it is wiser to attempt a safe shot that defends a potentially poor head than to attempt a risky shot which may open the way to a six if it fails to get the single for which you hope.

In four-a-side play the opposing leads each bowl – alternately – two bowls. It is a safe generalisation that if your two bowls finish closer to the jack on 12 or more of the 21 ends you will be doing a good job.

It will be an even better job if this is achieved on lengths of jack directed by your skip rather than on lengths chosen by you without thought of your three colleagues who will be following. Some skips do leave the choice of length to their leads, basing this on the tactical-pyschological idea that this will (a) ensure a two shots advantage and, so, (b) put the opposing four under immediate pressure. To some degree, this should depend on the skip's assessment of his own capabilities relative to that of the opposing skip.

If possible, it is preferable to have two bowls near to the jack than one very close and the other some way off. Having a lot of bowls near the jack does not guarantee that your four will actually score when the end is completed but it is a good form of insurance against your opponents running up a big score – say a four or even more – on any particular end.

Conversely, it may help you to a big score, either because they lose their accuracy momentarily or try to disturb your bowls instead of relying on bettering your best shot or shots.

Partly with this vision of his colleagues also bowling to positions close to the jack, it is advisable for a lead to seek mastery of one side of the rink – that is bowling on, say, the forehand going one way and on the backhand coming back the other way. This idea can also be extended by reverting to a couple of 'straight' bowls, that is minimum bias, for those days when you are playing as a lead. The value of a big bias lies in the ways one can curve the bowl round obstructions. In fours play the lead can never have more than two or, if he lost the previous end, three bowls near or on the jack when he delivers his second bowl.

So whether or not he is using 'straight' bowls, it is virtually unthinkable that he can be forced to change hands; a slight change of position on the mat or slightly different line of delivery should normally provide the way to avoid the nuisance bowl. The nuisance, anyway, is largely pyschological.

Bearing in mind the task of delivering your two bowls closer to the jack than your opponent's two, there may be occasions when the skip's directions hinder this object. One can be a call to fire, the other to bowl to the length jack that you, on the day, find most difficult.

This demands a special understanding, self confidence, and submission to your skip's reading of the eight bowlers on the rink as a whole rather than individuals – four of 'us', four of 'them'. In such cases banish thoughts of self from your mind, along with any inner judgement of your skip's tactics. Simply devote the whole of your mind and skill to the task of effectively meeting his requirements.

Perhaps after the match have a friendly exchange of views with him, during which you explain to him your problems and to reassure him that you tried to the limits of your skill to achieve his wishes. Seek also to discover his reasons for asking you to do that particular bidding of his.

The Number Two

Until fairly recent years the second bowler in a four was normally expected to fill in or cover up the holes left by the lead, as directed by the skip. If there were no holes, the skip would frequently signal for a positional bowl, as often as not to a blank space on the green rather than by the jack or another bowl.

This called for a somewhat special skill or, perhaps, temperament since most bowlers are happier when they can line up their delivery with a target or a 'sighter'. If you bowl frequently with this type of positional-minded skip, make time to tell him of your problems and ask him to be very specific when asking for such deliveries. Encourage him to point out useful 'sighter' bowls and to use his hand or handkerchief to indicate the precise position while you are aligning yourself for your delivery.

When Hong Kong won the fours event at the 1970 Commonwealth Games they changed the whole concept of play by a number two. The four comprised G. Delgado, A. Kitchell, R. da Silva and G. Souza and their approach was based on the concept that da Silva and Souza had to have room for maneouvre on any end which left the opposition with a favourable end after the first five or six bowls.

It has always been necessary for a number two to be effective with shots strong enough to travel a yard (a metre) or so beyond the jack if unimpeded by any other bowls. These 'yard on' shots are finesse-orientated, rather forceful, and are used primarily to 'trail the jack' from its position on the rink to one a foot or two farther back. The diagrams show a typical situation in which an accurately delivered bowl can convert a 'minus four' situation into 'plus four', a turnover of eight shots.

Note that in this situation the chances of a firing shot proving successful are inferior to those of the jack trailer. The jack is almost completely protected from any delivery that is too forceful to let the bias take effect.

There is also a chance that if the delivery is slightly off course, the bowl may gently push the bowl 1 out of the way while taking its position as the shot holder.

Kitchell's performance at Edinburgh and the intelligent way

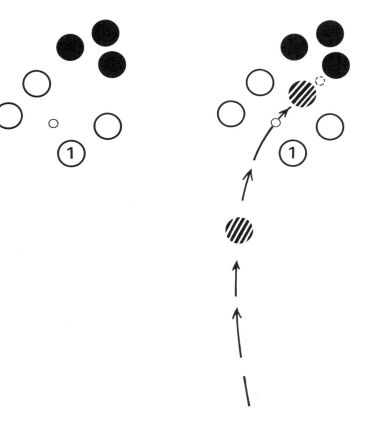

Ditch

Before

After

Diagram 15: A typical situation calling for a 'trailing the jack' shot. White is holding four shots.

Diagram 16: Black's delivery is right on target. It carries enough power to collect the jack and 'trail' it into a nest of his own bowls for a total of four shots.

Souza deployed him, judging impeccably whether to call for a positional shot, a trailer to clear the head or an outright drive to scatter the head, highlighted the Games. In fact, Hong Kong won 11 and drew one of the 13 matches they played to top the table with 23 out of a possible 26 points. In passing, a Hong Kong four containing only Souza of the 1970 team won the gold medal at the 1978 Games in Edmonton, Canada.

From all this it can be realised that a good number two must be versatile and strongly self disciplined. It used to be said that if one man of a four is weaker than the other three, put him at number two. Hong Kong killed that somewhat silly theory stone dead. Truth be told, there is really no room for a 'weaker' player in an ambitious four. In social play I would be inclined to let him skip, providing his theoretical knowledge - as distinct from his actual playing ability – sufficed to tell him when bowling into the head might do more harm than good.

No, in post-1970 bowls there is no room for a poorly performing or inadequately equipped, shotwise, number two.

Third Man

Apart from possessing all the shot repertoire of a number two, a third man should also be a master of the drive and a man temperamentally capable of maintaining unwavering nerve, control and accuracy under pressure.

Normally after the leads and number twos have completed their deliveries eight bowls will be clustered around the jack. The lead will have had yards of space in which to operate and the number two a few feet. The third man is frequently bowling with only a few inches of space to exploit. Irrespective of any demands this makes on technical ability, the mental pressure this can and does impose after three hours battling is significantly strong.

Because I realise that mental fitness is closely related to physical fitness, I am convinced that the third man and skip should take special care of their physical condition. Morning exercise may sound a little forbidding to a man in hs fifties who is bowling for pleasure. If he is normally a third man, improved fitness should make for better bowling which, in turn, must yield greater pleasure.

Third men bowl 95 per cent of the time under strict instructions for their skips; they have even less freedom of choice than their number two. Furthermore, when it is the skip's turn to deliver his two bowls, the third man takes over the skip's physical place behind the jack at the head.

Note my words 'physical position' because it is commonplace for skips to request from the mat an assessment and, sometimes, guidance on which shot to play.

It is incumbent on the third man to voice his beliefs but he must guard most carefully against understandably drifting into a state of offering unnecessary and uncalled for advice or information. He must, of all players, completely resist any conscious or semi-conscious assumption of the skip's duties. Particularly, never so much as by a word or gesture should he question his skip's tactics or instructions. A request 'may I try it on the backhand?' when told to play for a position or target using the forehand is about the limit.

Time and again the good team work and confidence of a compatable four overcomes four who are reputedly far superior but who bowl as individuals. A forward-looking, optimistic, understanding and technically skilled third man can contribute immensely to that good team work.

The positional jack-trailing or take-out shots of a third man differ little, if at all, from those of a number two. He will be called on from time to time to drive, maybe to crash the jack backwards into the ditch, perhaps to thump an opposing bowl out of a shot saving position, and quite often to kill a head on which the opponents hold many shots, thus forcing that end to be restarted.

Thus in any solitary practice session a third man should spend adequate time raising to high levels his strength and direction with jack-trailing shots and the power and accuracy of his driving. Because he must never neglect to practise drawing to jacks at all lengths from the mat, he should plan his bowls to allow more time for practice than a confirmed lead or number two. This may at times appear irksome but there is no substitute for well thought-out, intelligent practice for any man seeking to develop into a reliable match winner.

The Skip

Almost every one of the words devoted to third men holds good for skips. Technically and tactically they should approximate to perfection. Temperamentally they should combine the sense of adventure of those first men on the moon with the calculating thoroughness and reserve of an Eisenhower saying 'go' to an invasion of Europe. Above these, they must have a psychological insight into the minds and emotions of those they command plus the flexibility of character to command, demand, drive, encourage and, at all times, inspire others to give not 100 per cent but 110 per cent of what has always seemed their best.

No such ideal skip has ever existed so in selecting a skip, compromise must be part of the operation. Clearly he should be a thoroughly competent player but the intangibles just listed suggest that they can make one man a better skip than another who, as just a player, may be more skilful.

Certainly he must remain tranquil and unflappable under any kind of pressure – and pressure is ever present in the position he bowls, for on half the ends he plays his chances of success or failure are usually decided by distances of three or four inches (75 or 100 mm) one way or the other. And at a distance of, say, 35 yards (32 metres) from the jack, three inches (75 mm) is less than 1 per cent of the total distance.

So can you perform well under stress? Do you.possess unusual instincts for what other men are feeling, minute by minute? Can you accept the varying stings of Fate – good or bad – and treat them all just the same? Have you intense will to win, yet with an innate generosity that prevents disappointment destroying your form and self-confidence?

Answer 'yes' to all these and you are good skip material – but first learn to bowl well in all the other positions.

Do not permit yourself to be used as a skip too quickly. This happens in many clubs simply because the membership does not include sufficient skip-class material. Practice continuously to master all the shots. When they have been mastered, go on practising. Never let false pride permit you to be 'promoted' to skip. Deny yourself the ego-trip of such an important role and strive to master all the facets of higher performances in the position you normally play.

Remember, success is not measured by how well you appear to bowl but by the quantity and quality of the matches you win. What are the factors which differentiate victory from defeat?

Chapter Five
Strategy and Tactics

First be clear about the difference between strategy and tactics. The former is, essentially, the overall plan for winning the match. Tactics are the end-by-end methods used to implement the overall plan.

As an example, take Canada's win over the England four in the first ever World Championships. Seemingly, the Canadians did not fancy their chances of beating their probably more accurate opponents with finesse. Therefore they relied on aggression, with the drive as its main weapon.

So they bowled consistently for the jack itself without much concern about the general pattern of the head and the positional shots it suggested. But in all cases where an England player delivered a bowl to a particularly good position they immediately tried with their very next delivery to drive that bowl away. The ultimate in this came on an end when the England lead began one end with a bowl that settled on the jack. Without a moment's hesitation the Canadian lead unleashed a mighty drive which banged both the jack and the England bowl off the rink for a 'dead end'. On its replay Canada scored two shots. This and four other dead ends shattered English confidence and, when the match ended, had England snorting 'that wasn't bowls, it was skittles.'

Skittles or not, never before or since have I seen a 'dead end' forced by only the second bowl of an end. The final destruction of English morale fully justified Canada's overall strategy . . . and the immediate way tactics implemented the strategy at the slightest signs of coming danger.

One of the world's finest ever exponents of the drive was Scotland's Major Bob Cowan. His aggressive methods as an international skip were largely responsible for a now widely used strategy to reduce the morale-lowering destruction and aggravation of continuous driving.

The overall strategy is to keep the jack as far away as possible from the front of the mat and to avoid clustering bowls together around the jack. This 'streamlines' the target from a solidity which would be difficult to miss at short range down to three smaller units farther away from the mat. At longer range the only major success offered to a drive can depend on the deliverer hitting the jack, a small target at say, 35 yards (32 metres) from the mat (see diagrams 17 and 18).

Those using this strategy must possess ample skill in bowling to positions off the jack. Building heads with 'holes' for a drive to go through can be an extremely difficult operation for players who consistently use the jack as their target.

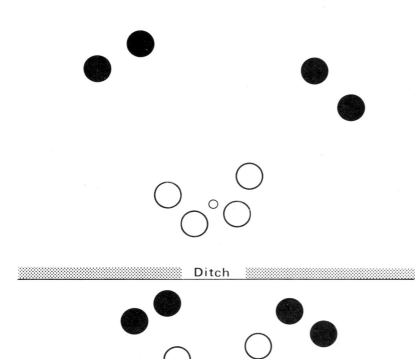

Diagram 17: White holds four shots but the jack is not at full length and the cluster offers a large target.

Ditch

Diagram 18: White again holds four shots but this time so positioned that the target is smaller; there is room for a drive to miss and go through.

Put the situation in reverse. Your opponents are using an 'open head' strategy and you are going through the holes with your drives. What do you do about it? The best answer is: never let yourself be in that situation. Practise your drawing to the jack and jack-trailing shots until, at worst, you can get near enough to the jack to hold your opponents to singles or twos. Meanwhile, do all in your power to keep your team on line with the jack for, at least, these can be driven on to the jack or into target clusters around the jack. Behind the jack a straight bowl can far more easily be brought into the count or a shot saving situation than one which is perfect for length but two or three feet wide of the jack. Use your most accurate drawer to the jack as your main chance to win an end, secure the jack and so enable you to switch to short jack tactics.

This emphasises to some degree the major aim of tactics which

47

is to deploy all one's strengths in attacks on the opposition's frailest weaknesses. The weakness may be temperamental, as one internationally famous bowler demonstrated in an English Indoor Singles Championship final some years ago.

Early in the final he built up a three shot position while his opponent delivered his first three bowls a yard or so behind the jack. The obvious play for the famed bowler was to put a saving bowl amongst those back three to protect himself against a four if the opponent successfully trailed the jack with the last bowl of the end.

Ignoring the obvious, he carefully drew a fourth shot in front of and slightly to the side of the jack. This left a clear run to the jack but with ample space for that last bowl to miss everything.

The reasoning was: 'if he does trail the jack and go through for a four I will be one behind as I am leading by three. He is an anxious type of person and that may spoil his delivery. If he does miss and lets me score four, I'll go seven shots ahead and I don't think he will recover.'

Fortune rewarded this clear tactical thinking. The fourth bowl went through the gaps, missed the jack and so the four was scored. As reasoned, this led to a decline in the deliverer's form and the famed bowler scored ten shots for the loss of only four in continuing his title-winning final.

In comparing the man-by-man comparisons of his men against the opposition, a skip must take into account his own skills compared with those of his opposite number. John Scadgell demonstrated this to perfection in the 1954 Commonwealth Games at Cardiff.

England and South Africa ended level so they had to contest a play-off for the gold and silver medals. In their league match England lead Norman King had substantially outbowled the South African lead using short length jacks, but the South African skip had an edge over Scadgell at this length. This caused problems, but during the match Scadgell discovered he was superior when bowling to full length jacks.

So before the play-off Scadgell explained the situation to King, called on him to help the strategy and asked him to concentrate on full length jacks even though this might reduce his personal effectiveness as a shot scorer.

A great bowler and tactician himself – two Commonwealth Games and one World Championship gold medals prove it – King played to these orders, Scadgell duly outbowled the South African skip, England won the play-off and the Championship.

Variations of length whenever in possession of the jack is a sound tactical move if your lead and number two are more accurate and touch-sensitive bowlers than their opposite numbers.

The majority of bowling greens are faster (the bowl trickles on further) over the four yards (3·7 metres) wide stretch by the ditches than over a four yards wide band ten yards (9·1 metres) in from the ditches. This is caused mainly by hardening from the constant trampling of players around heads, changing ends, delivering their bowls and so on.

Refer to diagram 19 of a 40 yards by 40 yards (36 by 36 metres) green. The shaded area shows the four yards wide band of surface hardened by trampling.

Line A shows how a 28-yard (25·6-metre) length jack delivered from a mat moved up the green is in the middle of the faster running band.

Line B shows that a jack 28 yards from a mat well back on the green is on a slower running part of the green.

Thus a bowl delivered at **x** miles per hour will trickle longer on A, therefore curving more, than one delivered at a similar speed on line B. So the leads and number twos with superior sensitivity of touch should be able to adapt far more easily to these slight changes of line and strength than their opponents.

The skip who is always seeking to take the initiative is usually more exciting and inspiring than one who is more conventional in his tactics. This in itself, and used discreetly, is also a form of strategy for any methods which spread cheer and confidence, two important pyschological facets of success-achieving are valuable.

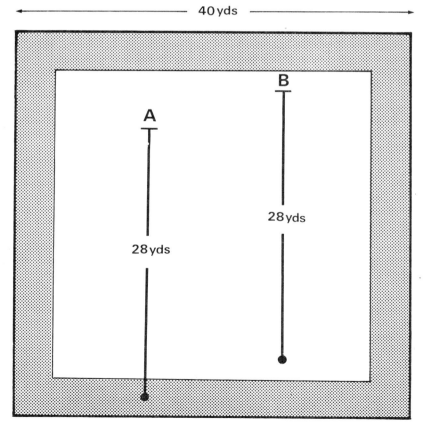

Diagram 19: The shaded area shows the band of grass four yards wide around the green made harder and faster than any similar band nearer to the centre of the green by trampling of feet.

Chapter Six
Concentration, Attitudes and Practice

Every game presents special problems concerning concentration. One common to all ball games is the short time one is directly concerned in the action relative to the total time one is on the playing area.

For example, in tennis the ball is hit back and forth in rallies for only about 20 per cent of the total time, as registered by the 'match began' and 'match ended' entries on the umpire's score sheet – yet even this 20 per cent is enormous when compared with a bowler in a fours match. Each man of the eight (four against four) has no direct effect on the action for 98 per cent of the time.

Clearly then, he needs two types of concentration to cope effectively with the differing active-inactive roles.

Some bowlers, former international Graham Howard is an example, concentrate fully on every aspect of each bowl delivered by all eight players. Others, they include former England singles champion Jim Davidson, quietly observe the action but without allowing themselves to become emotionally involved. A few like former British Isles champion Billy Tate, sometimes turn their backs on the action, waiting until each bowl has come to a stop before reappraising the general position at the head. This certainly eliminates the 'will it, won't it, oh, its missed' palpitations as- sociated with the passage of each bowl down the green. However, such switching on and off is not too easy to control. Each player must discover his own system.

Nevertheless, electronic stop watch measurements of the time intervals of players stepping on the mat and then the actual moments of release emphasise this need for the two distinct kinds of concentration, one applied, the other of passive observation. The former is concerned with the actual delivery, the latter with how concentration may be sustained when a player is not actually bowling. Figures show how important this is.

The direct influence any bowler may impose on a game is limited to the time he steps on the mat and then releases his bowl. Prior to that he can analyse and assess the situation, decide what he should do about it and begin mentally rehearsing the delivery he will make.

One bowl later the position may be changed, so necessitating a reappraisal and further analysis and mental rehearsal.

Once the bowl leaves his hand there is nothing more he can do with it. His control and accuracy may be good, bad or indifferent. He can use 'feed back' to improve his next shot but as for the bowl now an inch or so on its way towards the head, nothing can be done. The bowler's direct ability to change the game with that bowl has ended. My extensive measurements show that this time delay between stepping on the mat and then releasing a bowl is predominantly around five to seven seconds, though the full scale ranged from 2·9 to 15·24 seconds.

Taking 6 seconds as average, a bowler can directly influence the game as follows:

	Number of bowls	Time of influence	Average length of match	Time not directly in play
Pairs	84	8·40 min	210 min	201·60 min
Triples	54	5·40 min	190 min	184·60 min
Fours	42	4·20 min	210 min	205·80 min

In approximate percentages, then, the direct influence figures are 4, $2\frac{3}{4}$ and 2 per cent, the percentages of time when the bowler is not in use are, pairs 96, triples $97\frac{1}{4}$, fours 98 per cent.

How best to pace concentration during those long off-mat spells can now be realised in its full importance.

Seemingly, it is essential to observe the way in which the game is developing, the pace of the green, any changes brought about by sun, rain or wind. Particular runs should be noted, realising that a 'run' for one bowl over a piece of flat green may vary from that of a bowl of differing composition, weight, dimensions and shape.

Here it may be noted that some bowlers – David Bryant and Norma de la Motte are two examples – make it a duty to know precisely the make, size, weight, bias and individual idiosyncrosies of the bowls used by their opponents.

Such studies, backed by a thorough analysis of the various shots by the opponents, are vital to good performance and concentration.

Left: Former British Isles singles champion, Bill Tate, with the trophy. He controls his concentration by relaxing and looking away from the game while his opponet bowls. Then he studies the head, appraises the situation and brings full concentration to bear on the shot he plays to exploit that situation.

Above: A fours match takes, on average, 210 minutes, so it is physically tiring. Those six bowlers would have been well advised to watch the play while sitting down. Few bowlers husband their energies.

Yet it is also true that concentration ebbs and flows in a rhythm related to the basic personality structure of an individual, especially in the place along the introversion – extraversion scale of that individual.

The skill lies in knowing one's own capabilities and in developing through training – consciously or subconsciously – systems for achieving peaks of concentration each time one steps on the mat.

Certainly, some form of detachment seems necessary; the bowler who 'lives' with the deliverer of every single wood that travels the green is running a serious risk of mental and neural exhaustion towards the end of a close match.

On the other hand, chatting away on the bank with friends will, almost certainly, run concentration down too far for it to be raised to its effective peak for delivery.

Relaxation and a disciplined unconcern about whether each bowl travelling the green will be good, bad, indifferent, unlucky or an outrageous fluke should be developed. Full realisation that one can do nothing about it – what is to be will be – helps.

Yoga breathing helps self control enormously. As your time to deliver approaches begin controlled and conscious inhaling and exhaling, culminating in a deep, controlled inward breath leading up to the start of your swing, followed by gentle, smooth exhaling in rhythm with your relaxed delivery. This needs practice.

At other times a slight variation of this type of breathing is advantageous. Be conscious of your breathing but without consciously controlling it. Aim over a period of time to increase the depth of your breathing and to reduce its tempo.

These techniques should help tranquility, reduce the spoiling effects of nervousness and improve concentration. However, there are physiological reasons for declining concentration. Chewing gum helps in some respects though I must confess to a personal dislike of champing jaws.

Tiredness reduces the sugar content in one's blood and this, in turn, diminishes the brain's powers of awareness. In bowls this means a reduction in a player's ability to comprehend the full implications of a head, even if his execution of the shot he attempts is up to his best standards.

Special foods and drink have been developed, most of them based on glucose, some with mineral additives. In my opinion, high intensity glucose syrup supplemented by potassium and minerals is best and such a product is available under the brand name 'Dynamo'.

Finally, be reminded that even the mathematical, scientific genius Albert Einstein had first to master his multiplication tables. In bowls the parallel is 'keep your eyes on the green'. On this simple base you can develop the more advanced, positive techniques advocated here . . . and probably with practice and experience produce some of your own.

A good example of absolute concentration. This player's whole attitude is bent on the shot about to be produced.

Nature abhors a vacuum, including one in the mind. Ensure yours is filled with useful, positive thoughts and plans.

When bowling ensure that you maintain a steady tempo for stepping on the mat and delivering your bowl. Banish like the plague the common 'three seconds for the first bowl, five seconds for the second, eight for the third and sixteen for the fourth' pattern so often seen.

With well regulated concentration you will increase your chances of achieving maximum effectiveness with every bowl you send down. Elsie Wilkie did at Wellington and, again, at Worthing. She won the world singles championship each time.

Well regulated concentration is significantly helped by well adjusted attitudes towards the game as a whole and winning or losing in particular. In developing a good attitude I believe the search for perfection, with the better performances which in-evitably come with progress towards it, is superior to the excessive motivation for winning found in many bowlers. Such motivation leads too often to anxiety and nervousness.

One needs to differentiate nervousness from deeper seated anxiety. Anxiety is the result of looking backwards to what has happened in the past and projecting it forward to the future, so reducing the power to concentrate all one's efforts and skills on the immediate. Nervousness is glandular and shows you are geared for action.

Now it is all very well to pontificate about concentrating only on the shot about to be tried but that does not take into account human frailties. Far better, then, to discover and develop practical techniques which can be brought into operation through practice and application. One of the best is fragmentation.

Normally games players tend to think in terms of large parcels: 'I must win this end', 'survive this over', 'win my service' and so on. Or they go to the other extreme and become swamped in the minutia of technique: 'see my feet are right, check the grip, make sure the swing back is straight' and so on, ad infinitum.

Inevitably they suffer from technical inhibition and, far from performing better, lose the best of which they are capable. The ideal is to find a suitable balance between the eagerness of com-petition and the relaxation which alone allows nerves and muscles to function efficiently.

The object of practice is to formulate 'nerve grooves' which allow an action, in bowls a mode of delivery, to become virtually automatic. The parallel is driving a motor car. Once one has become proficient the car virtually steers itself while the ex-perienced driver sits in a state of relaxed concentration which permits instant correction of anything untoward.

This state of 'trusting the body' is the ideal one should seek in bowling or performing any other technical sports movement. The mind should be the ever alert but relaxed watchdog ready to give a little touch here, apply a little brake there and so on.

Once this state of technical consistency has been achieved the mind becomes free to scheme objectively about factors significantly more important to winning or losing. Anxiety can be controlled or banished by, say, fragmentation.

Taking a simple example, in fours play each man delivers two bowls per end. It is usual for him to concentrate on each one individually but to consider it in relationship to the end as a whole. This tends to produce a succession of anxiety peaks. Mentally it is better to stand a little outside oneself, as it were, and take a broader view of the situation.

If a player (or set of players, e.g. a triple) wins every end by scoring a single he cannot be beaten and victory eventually falls into his lap like a ripe plum falling off a tree.

Though in the case of, say, fours this necessitates a team effort, the team is only as good as its individual members. Team or individual? I recall Herb Elliott's summary when asked this question. One of the greatest runners in history, he replied 'the only time I think about Australia is when I am standing on the rostrum and they start playing bloody Waltzing Matilda'. One thinks of the team but one should strive with every ounce of determination to achieve one's personal best.

When a skip is involved it is usual for his unit to bowl to his orders. Yet in so obeying, each bowler is, in reality, engaged in a battle with his opposite number. In the case of leading, the outcome is normally apparent from who holds the shot after the first four bowls. The number two may not enjoy such a clear cut picture, especially if he is being used in the head-clearing way featured by the Hong Kong gold medallists at the 1970 Commonwealth Games.

Yet it remains a personal battle which an anxious bowler can mentally isolate from the contest as a whole and so spare himself much of the anxiety which can arise from the trauma suffered by other members of the four.

He can further fix his mind in the present by thinking in terms of having two bowls and determining that one of them will precisely produce the shot demanded by the skip.

Carrying this idea further, it is possible to sub-divide the 21 ends into seven 'little' matches, each of three ends, in which victory goes to the man who 'wins' two – or all three – of them.

All these techniques are designed to obliterate memories of past failures and future hopes so that every ounce of mental energy and toughness can be expended on the immediate contest.

Rationalising, only divine intervention can change what has already happened and ordinary mortals cannot foretell the future, so that it is pointless and stupid to waste energy dwelling on either. The only moment to backtrack is immediately after your bowl has gone just wrong. Then consider exactly what happened, correct it in your mind, mentally make a corrected delivery – the more vivid the imagined delivery and outcome the better – and

Three different levels of concentration. The bowler at the far end has focused full attention on his delivery while his skip, kneeling, is watching to see where the bowl will stop before assessing the situation. So will the opposing skip, standing, but first he is studying the path of the bowl in case his player will need guidance about direction.

then forget it, thinking instead positively of what will next be needed and exactly how you will achieve it.

This system is capable of development by any captain who is determined to lift his team to greater heights and one valuable aid is 'Hazard Training.' To do this he should arrange a match between his team and a team of opponents who are in some way rivals. The rivals are instructed to be as bothersome, difficult etc as possible. They can be encouraged to move at the head, to walk up the green when their opposite numbers are on the mat, to crowd from behind, to talk, clap etc when their opponents are bowling, to get the score wrong, to displace bowls in the head, to chase bowls noisily and, generally, to try their utmost to break the concentration of the team under test.

Each 'incident' should be considered immediately by the bowlers immediately affected and with the captain present. Attitudes and ways to behave should be talked out quietly and with freedom from tension; experience of this form of training of world-ranking tennis stars has proved to me that once they have developed the intellectual understanding of how to cope with a situation through unpressurised practice of it, the attitude generally carries through to real match reproductions. Of course they sometimes lapse; emotions during intense competition run high but rehearsal greatly eliminates the unknown aspects which are so damaging to tranquility. Tranquility is so important in forming or maintaining sound attitudes, especially in important contests.

Turn from Bowls for a moment and consider instead the line up for the final of the 800 metres in the Olympic Games. As, in your imagination, you run your eyes down the contestants you notice that all are very similar in height and even more so in build.

Your neighbour is an expert in the training of such men. He will tell you that all have trained very similarly, seven days a week, for the previous two or three years and that their best times over the distance vary by less than two per cent. Theoretically a dead heat between all of them is not too improbable.

Yet how differently it all works out once the gun has gone. One or two may run better than ever in their lives, another two, say, around par and the rest will fall far short of their best-ever times.

In a nutshell, roughly 50 per cent of the finalists will perform appreciably below their best despite the fact that they will have spent two or three years training and competing in championships in which they have established themselves as the best in their countries.

They will have been the subjects of intense publicity, coached and trained with immense skill and yet, on this day of days, this one special day in 1,000, their performances will be relatively poor.

Remembering that all follow almost identical training patterns and routines and have similar physical similarities, these great variations in performance must derive from some non-physical force. Probably there are a number of terms that can be applied to this force. In general, however, it is safe to attribute the failure to anxiety, nervousness, psychology, or lack of a big match temperament.

The purpose of that analysis is to identify with the failure of England's finest bowlers to justify themselves in recent International Team Championship matches. Some reports stressed the failure of the number twos and third men to stand up to pressure. It is reasonable, therefore, to consider the failure in the light of the Olympic analogy; this analogy is based on fact and is not a figment of someone's imagination.

It may safely be assumed that every one of the 24 men was eager to bowl as never before. Shakespeare may have written 'my Kingdom for a horse.' Most of those concerned would, I fancy, have traded a year's salary for 42 dead touchers per match. In other words, all were strongly motivated.

And so to the first clue to the failures. Round about the turn of the century Messrs Yerkes and Dodson founded the now well authenticated pyschological law which bears their name. Put simply, this shows that the more complicated an operation is, the more it is inhibited by strong motivation.

Is delivering a bowl a complicated operation? Viewed casually, the answer may seen 'no'. When considered in detail as in this book, delivery is an intricate operation in which the details of mechanics must be related to the intricacies of the green and the situation at the head. The excessive motivation of the match will be an ever present hazard which is liable to intensify as each poor bowl increases the wish and intention of its deliverer to achieve something better next time.

Summarising, excessive motivation spoils performance which increases anxiety which intensifies motivation which mars performance . . . and so on. What, then, can be done about it?

In the short term, not a lot. In the long term, a great deal if the reasons are understood and the remedies practised assiduously.

Firstly, outward manifestations of anxiety should be banished. Any lead or number two who chases his bowl up the green should immediately be stopped by the skip and persistence in the habit after being told should result in automatic rejection by the selection committee until such time as the bowler ends the habit.

Note that this is not because of any wasting of time. Just possibly such action could be wrong. The Scots are inveterate chasers up the green but, from observations, this appears to be because they wish to enjoy to the full the pleasure, satisfaction, what have you, of the bowl snuggling into its target position. Additionally, they reveal much stronger signs of extroversion than the English and so their 'showmen' content is more strongly marked.

Watching English bowlers chasing up the green leaves any psychologically attuned observer with a strong impression of the deliverer's anxiety.

Chasing the bowl, far from alleviating the anxiety, is likelier to reinforce it, so increasing the pressure. Recent research in America suggests that when we act or look anxious, even if we are not, we start off a tiny chain reaction which eventually develops the appearance into the reality.

Calmness and tranquility are the impressions given by Mrs Irene Molyneux, a much-capped England international — impressions which banish anxiety from her team, and indeed can eventually prevent anxiety in herself.

Conversely, then, to look calm and tranquil is to begin a pyschological process that can, eventually, rid us of inner turmoil.

Consider now the effect bowl-chasing and other manifestations of anxiety impose on other members of the four. Even if only slightly, your obvious lack of self confidence will be communicated to them. They will begin to suffer, if only slightly, from anxiety and they will remember this next time you deliver, either subconsciously or consciously.

So when the deliverer next steps on the mat, their anxiety will be re-transmitted back to him. War time research into bomber crews by the RAF substantiates what was once pure theory but may soon be accepted as fact if recent American research is fully authenticated. Briefly, this research, it is claimed, has established a physical explanation for thought transference which is in some way akin to the propogation and reception of radio waves.

The 'do not', then, is to show any outward signs of anxiety or nervousness but this 'negative' must be replaced by a 'positive'. That 'positive' is mental rehearsal backed by vivid imagination. Its practice demands considerable effort and concentration but this, in itself, is a valuable antidote to nervousness.

Firstly, though, fully understand that mental rehearsal is a thoroughly proven fact and a technique used by world champions in many fields. Assume you have just delivered your first bowl of an end. Instead of standing anxiously to deliver the second, think strongly of that delivery. If it is a good one, strive to recapture the feeling. If the bowl goes wrong, calmly work out why, if necessary watching your opponent's shot to help in analysing *your* fault. Be calm and positive about this. *On no account think negatively: 'I'm bowling badly to-day'.*

All that has happened is that you have made a technical error in delivery or have misjudged the situation. As you step on the mat, make the correction in your mind. Then, before actually loosing your bowl, stand and imagine it going up the green in exactly the way you intend. Make the mental picture as vivid as you possibly can. Perhaps you will be accused of taking a long time over your delivery. No matter. Unless the umpire specifically tells you to hurry up, make this mental rehearsal – based on previous objective, corrective analysis – an automatic part of your routine. Then, when that picture is stamped on your mind, deliver your bowl.

Let me emphasise that adoption of this system demands intense concentration but that concentration, in itself, is a tremendous method of harnessing for good any nervousness which hitherto has marred performance. Nervousness shows one is stimulated for action; that the normal adrenalin is flowing, so preparing body and mind for 'fight or flight'. The skill of the successful lies in harnessing that nervousness. This is a matter of technique.

When assailed by 'butterflies in the tummy' or other manifestations of nervousness, say to yourself 'good, I'm really keyed up for action to-day.' Use your will power to obliterate all thoughts of winning or losing. Use deep breathing to help your calmness when others are bowling. When your turn draws near make your breathing more conscious.

If stray thoughts or fears sneak into your mind, do not pursue them. Just think about calmness and start mentally rehearsing your next delivery. Try to relax while making your mental picture as real as possible.

Take time out to walk up the green to study the head if you need more time to establish calmness. Think of what you have to do, take an extra deep breath and as you start to exhale, let your delivery flow with your muscles and joints as relaxed as possible.

This technique improves with practice. Add to it a true love of competition in which you hope your opponent is in good form so that you may contest a fine game in which you can prove yourself better than him at his best.

If you win, act graciously. If you lose, be generous in spirit to your conqueror while you resolve within yourself to put right your mistakes so you can beat him next time.

The ladder of success is made from rungs which are mostly defeats. Changing them to victories is absorbing and satisfying – so satisfying that when players climb to the top they often experience a feeling of anti-climax. The journey has been so much more pleasurable than the arrival.

My book aims to ease that journey for you so that it is even more enjoyable. As for your arrival at your ambition, you can take care of that yourself, but when you get there please drop me a line to tell me all about it.

Chapter Seven
Crown Green Bowling

There is a story heard sometimes in bowling circles that it is extremely difficult to find pieces of flat ground large enough to put down a traditional, full size Bowls green, in the northern areas of England and Wales.

So the game is mostly played on either sub-standard flat greens or, more popular in specific counties, on greens which are by design anything from eight to eighteen inches higher in their centres than at their banks. This game has its own name, Crown Green Bowls. As BBC Television promotes and transmits nationally a specific tournament each year, the difference between the IBB flat green code and that of the crown green game are now much better known than before the BBC's intervention.

The rule governing the size of a crown green is far more elastic than the equivalent in the IBB rules. It may vary from 30 to 60 yards (27·4 to 54·9 metres) square though many adhere to the 40 by 40 yards of most flat greens. The green slopes upwards to the centrally raised centre - the crown – which is anything from eight to eighteen inches higher than the four boundary sides. This, allied to a natural tendency for such greens to be a little bumpier than flat greens introduces extra hazards to those who play.

Singles are predominant though Pairs matches are sometimes to be seen. Whether it be singles or pairs, each player delivers only two bowls per end. Thus the maximum number of bowls facing the man who makes the last 'cast' – the word used instead of 'deliver' – is three in singles or seven in pairs. Thus there is scarcely any of the intricate juggling for position that is inherent when, as in flat green championships play, there are eight bowls per end in singles, sixteen per end in pairs and fours and eighteen per end in triples.

So the crown green game is based almost exclusively on drawing to the jack, a skill made difficult to acquire because of the uneven green, the general rules and the use of a biassed jack instead of the pure spherical jack of the IBB game.

One of the four sides embraces near its centre the official entrance to the green and in amateur matches play must begin within three yards of that entrance. In the professional version of Crown Green Bowls play begins at the centre. The professionals use a mat only four inches (102 mm) in diameter and one foot must remain in contact with it throughout the 'cast'. Amateurs use a larger 'footer' – the crown green word used instead of mat - which is 12 inches (305 mm) in diameter.

As in the flat green game, the object is to 'cast' one's bowls so both finish nearer to the jack than those of the opponent. The standard game is won by the first player reaching 21 but many matches and tournaments break away from this standard, using any number between 11 and 41 as game.

There are no rules governing the bowls used and in 1968 the governing body was forced to clip the wings of a few enthusiasts who occasionally used a jack as a bowl. However, physical dynamics dictate that the most satisfactory weight lies between two and a half and three pounds approximately and of a somewhat smaller diameter than the flat green variety. In terms of bias, anything goes, but one approximating to $2\frac{1}{4}$ (in IBB terms) is the most effective. However, each match and green presents situations which can be exploited or overcome by a special bowl and it is customary for top flight crown green players to carry many sets of two in the boots of their cars; as many as 16 has been known.

The other major difference between the two codes is in the direction of play. In the IBB game each set of bowlers play on a clearly defined strip of ground (rink) stretching up and down the green.

In crown green bowls the jack may be thrown in any direction. To be 'live' it must be at least 21 yards (19·2 metres) from the footer, not less than three yards (2·7 metres) from the central clearly marked area of the green and it is not a 'mark' if both jack and footer are less than four yards (3·7 metres) from the same edge of the green. On heavy greens a player is allowed to claim a maximum 56 yards (51·2 metres) diagonally on a 40 yards (36·6 metres) square green, thus neutralising any advantage of brute strength he may consider his opponent enjoys; the skills of drawing to the jack are carefully safeguarded in crown green bowls.

Since play can and does take place in every conceivable direction and it is customary, as in flat green play, to play many games simulataneously on a green, the picture to a casual, unknowing onlooker is of utter chaos. Collisions of all kinds inevitably take place and the rules cover all such eventualities.

The use of a biassed jack on a sloping green opens up ways of presenting opponents with ever varying conditions of play. Throwing the jack so that its bias supplements the slope of the green sets up a wide sweep situation, called a 'round peg'. When the jack is cast towards the centre with its bias working against the slope it is known as a 'square peg'.

An astute tactician who notes before play that his opponent is using highly polished, wide sweep bowls can, if he is also an accurate player, make it impossible for that opponent to keep his bowls on the green by consistently casting the jack so that it and the footer are parallel with an edge of the green and just above the four yards minimum. By watching telecasts of matches or, better, by playing oneself, a better understanding of the complexities of this subtle version of bowls can be obtained.

It is subtle because the sheer power plays (firing shots) of the flat green, IBB game are seldom used; often an entire match will

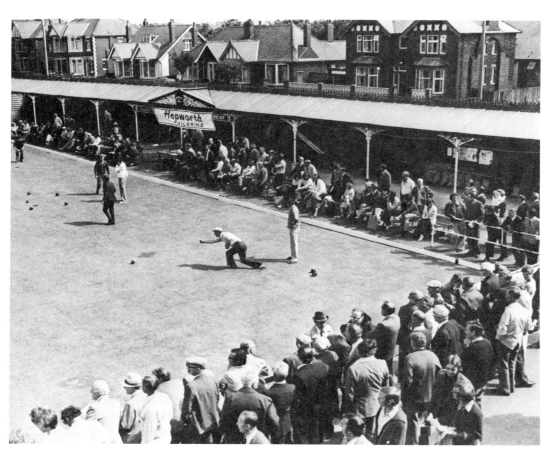

Crown green bowling in 1977 at one of the most famous centres of the sport in the north of England, the Waterloo Hotel, Blackpool.

be completed without any of the participants using a firing shot. Except for the dubious chance of disturbing the confidence of a bowler who specialises in accurate drawing to 21 yard jacks, the only 'percentage' use of the firing shot is when the opponent has cast his two bowls near to the jack in virtually unbeatable positions. Then the firing shot must be so powerful that the curving effect of the bias and the crown are neutralised but the use of such power must, in itself, mitigate against the accuracy needed to shatter a small target anything from 21 to 56 yards away.

Crown green devotees swear their version of bowls is superior to all others, an attitude strongly countered by their contemporaries who stick to the IBB code. One or two clubs, notably the Tally Ho club in Birmingham, offer the best of two worlds by having two greens, one for each code. Thus members may be devoted to one or the other but can relax when they wish by taking a quiet turn to the, maybe, despised alternative. From watching casually one or two competitors in the annual EBA Championships who also play a certain amount of crown green bowls I have gathered a slight impression that the disciplines they comply with have helped their accuracy, but I stress this is only a subjective thought.